Strategies of Resistance
& 'Who are the Trotskyists?'

Socialist Resistance would be glad to have readers' opinions of this book, its design and translations, and any suggestions you may have for future publications or wider distribution.

Our books are available at special quantity discounts to educational and non-profit organizations, and to bookstores.

To contact us, please write to Resistance Books at: PO Box 62732, London, SW2 9GQ, Britain, email: contact@socialistresistance.org or visit: http://socialistresistance.org

© International Institute for Research and Education 2009

Published by Socialist Resistance, 2009
Second printing, 2010

Printed in Britain by LightningSource

ISBN 978-0-902869-86-8
EAN 9780902869868

Published by the International Institute for Research and Education as a double issue, number 42/43 of the Notebooks for Study and Research.

'Who are the Trotskyists' is translated by Nathan Rao, with the kind permission of Presses Universitaires de France, from *Les trotskysmes* by Daniel Bensaïd, "Que sais-je ?" n° 3629, second ed. 2002. The other items appear with the kind permission of *International Viewpoint*.

Strategies of Resistance
& 'Who are the Trotskyists?'

Daniel Bensaïd

International Institute for Research and
Education, Amsterdam

Resistance Books, London

DANIEL BENSAÏD

Contents

Preface

We live in interesting times – certainly that is true for the present moment.

Millions around the world had already been mobilizing against the new variant of capitalism associated with the term "globalization" – refusing to accept the notion that "there is no alternative" to the ravages of the market economy, insisting on a "globalization-from-below" uniting across borders activists against war and imperialism, against environmental and cultural degradation, against multi-faced violations of human rights, against poverty and exploitation.

Conservative and neo-conservative triumphalism was already wearing thin, as had been the case with the varieties of liberal and social-democratic reformism. The vibrancy of anarchist challenges to the status quo were already indicating their limitations, with some intellectuals and activists pushing for something more coherent, more able to provide a sustained and potentially successful challenge to what we are up against. From the margins some were already pressing for new considerations of the Marxist tradition, for the resources to be found in the ideas of Rosa Luxemburg, even suggesting the imminence of "Lenin's return."

And now we are treated to the spectacle of "neo-liberal" disgrace, with collapsing financial markets sending some of the most conservative of "free-market" economists reeling in shock and disbelief, with their political representatives scurrying for "socialistic" government regulation and nationalization. There seems to be general agreement across the political spectrum that capitalism is entering a terrible crisis, and that many of us will suffer for it. For increasing numbers of people around the world, life will get worse.

Daniel Bensaid's challenging survey *Who are the Trotskyists* comes at an appropriate moment. It is a gift to activists reaching for some historical perspective that may provide hints as to where we might go from here. Embracing and sharing the revolutionary socialist political tradition associated with Leon Trotsky, Bensaid is not simply a thoughtful radical academic or perceptive left-wing intellectual – though he is certainly both – but also one of the foremost leaders of an impressive network of activists, many of them seasoned by innumerable struggles. This is commonly known as the Fourth International.

This entity sought to provide an alternative to the Social-Democratic "moderation" and opportunistic adaptation to capitalism represented by the Socialist International (the Second International), and to the vicious authoritarianism and cynical manipulations represented by the Stalin's stranglehold on the Communist International (the Third International). But while it was hopefully labeled "the World Party of Socialist Revolution," it never was able to match the mass parties and influence of the Second and Third Internationals. And yet its political perspectives embraced the revolutionary politics of Marx and Engels, of Rosa Luxemburg, and of the Bolshevik Revolution led by Lenin and Trotsky. There is no doubt that there are compelling qualities in these perspectives for those who want to change the world.

This is why, in 1938 (after several years of preparation), a handful of revolutionary socialists joined with Trotsky to establish this Fourth International. Its purpose was to end all forms of human oppression and degradation, to create a cooperative commonwealth in which the free development of each person is the condition for the free development of all. But fascism, Stalinism, imperialism, and war were then engulfing the world. So it was a brave project to which these comrades were committing themselves, and many of them were destroyed in the high tide of authoritarianism and violence.

The Marxist program of liberation, to which they were dedicated, was itself the culmination of two things — on the one hand the rich intellectual labor of those engaged in the passionate and scientific study of society, on the other hand the accumulation of lessons learned through the struggles of working people and the oppressed. This body of theory reflects the energies and creative efforts, in many cases the tears and blood, of our brothers and sisters in the workers' movement who went before us. This program of the Fourth International remains alive only if we refuse to worship it as a holy relic but instead connect it with the realities and struggles of our own lives, of our own time.

In advanced capitalist countries, in the so-called underdeveloped countries exploited by foreign corporations and imperialist interventions, in post-capitalist countries with nationalized, planned economies that are weighed down by bureaucratic rule— in what were seen as "the three sectors of world revolution" – the Fourth International offered what has come to be known as the transitional program. This held that revolutionaries in each country must be involved in the immediate economic and democratic struggles of working people, of women, of oppressed national and ethnic and racial groups, of students and youth. It also insisted that the struggles for immediate and winnable demands, to better the condition of people in the here-and-now, are absolutely necessary. But it recognized that certain basic problems will only be solved when the resources of the economy are socially owned and democratically controlled for the purpose of meeting human needs. That's what socialism is.

This could, according the new International's founding document, only be won by overcoming the powerful resistance of capitalists, imperialists, dictators, and bureaucrats — those who want to stay on top and keep the rest of us "in our place." But that's precisely what must be changed. Therefore, intertwined with these immediate demands, there must be transitional demands which make sense to masses of people in the present (and which people maybe prepared to fight for) but which cannot be realized under the present system.

For example, everyone has a right to a good job, to a good and full education, to decent housing and good health care. And since working people keep the country running, the country should be run in the interests of, and under the control of, working people— the majority. Out of such reasonable ideas as these, and out of the lived experience of people in specific situations, transitional demands must be fashioned. When masses of people are prepared to fight for such demands, a socialist revolution can happen.

Such revolutions don't happen automatically. They take place only if people work very hard and very consciously to make them happen. The Fourth International exists to help build and strengthen organizations of such people throughout the world. This revolutionary internationalism is not simply a worthy ideal. It is a practical necessity. The insights and defeats and victories gained by labor and liberation struggles in one country will profoundly influence what is understood and what can be accomplished in other countries. The Fourth International has offered such distinctive perspectives as these:

 o The theory of permanent revolution, linking together democratic and socialist revolutions in an internationalist framework.

 o The revolutionary insight that humanity faces a choice between socialism or barbarism.

 o The insistence that democracy must be at the heart of the working class and revolutionary movements and at the heart of the socialist goal.

o The knowledge that the tactic of the united front must be utilized to draw people together against the assaults of capitalism and reaction, as well as to test the capacities of contending left-wing currents.

o The transitional program for socialist revolution.

The Fourth International has made unique contributions by basing itself on the totality of these perspectives, and also – in line with the dialectical and critical method of Marx's own "scientific socialism" – by being able to absorb new lessons.

This means not simply the self-transformation coming from feminist and environmental and other insights, or the expanding and deepening of our knowledge under the impact of evolving social and economic realities, or the enrichment of perspectives coming from engagement with political currents and struggles that have emerged outside of our own specific Trotskyist tradition.

Absorbing new lessons certainly involves all of these things – but in addition, it involves the critical re-examination of our own theoretical and historical tradition, in the light of our own accumulating experiences and insights. And this is where Daniel Bensaid's important reflection on Trotskyisms fits in.

Daniel Bensaid emerged decades ago as a leader of the French section of the Fourth International, the Ligue Communiste Révolutionnaire (LCR). Coming from the "generation of '68" – the layer of young revolutionary activists of the 1960s – he blends an impressive intellectual sophistication with a refreshing inclination for revolutionary audacity, and with activist commitments which have not faded over the decades.

In the tradition of Ernest Mandel, Bensaid has reached for the continuing relevance of revolutionary Marxism not only in the battlegrounds of academe (as a professor of philosophy and author of such works as Marx for Our Times), but even more in the battlegrounds of social and political struggles against the oppressive and lethal realities of capitalist "globalization."

In this particular work – succinct, crackling with insights and fruitful provocations – Bensaid surveys the history of his own political tradition. We are not presented with a catechism, but with a set of informative and critical-minded reflections and notes. We don't have to agree with all he says. I certainly question his taking issue with Trotsky over whether or not Lenin was essential for the triumph of the Russian Revolution (Trotsky says definitely yes, Bensaid suggests maybe not). Nor am I satisfied when he gives more serious consideration to the dissident current in U.S. Trotskyism of Max Shachtman and James Burnham (both of whom ended up supporting U.S. imperialism in Vietnam) than to the tradition connected with James P. Cannon (which played a role in building a powerful movement that helped end the Vietnam war).

On the other hand, Bensaid makes no pretension of providing a rounded historical account of world Trotskyism, or even a scholarly account of the more limited issues that he does take up.* He emphasizes that "this essay is based on personal experience" and is focused on what he views as "the major debates" within the movement. And one is especially struck by the excellent point he makes in his introduction regarding the necessity of understanding the varieties of Trotskyism around the world in their distinctive cultural and national specificities. Little sense can be made of Trotskyism if it is not related to the actual social movements and class struggles of various parts of the world, and to the left-wing-labor sub-cultures, in which it had meaning.

The fact remains that Bensaid offers us a thoughtful, stimulating, valuable political intervention which leaves the reader with a sense of Trotskyism's history and ideas and diverse manifestations – and also a sense of their relevance for the struggles of today and tomorrow. For younger activists beginning to get their bearings, and for veterans of the struggle who are thinking through the questions of where we have been and where to go from here, this is an important contribution.

Paul Le Blanc

Who are the Trotskyists?

Translator's note

Where possible, I have tracked down existing English-language translations of the writings of Leon Trotsky and various figures from the Trotskyist movement quoted in the original French-language edition of this book. The same goes for the Fourth International documents and resolutions excerpted in the book. While I was able to find a few items in my own personal library, I relied heavily on the *Leon Trotsky Internet Archive*[1] and the *Toward a History of the Fourth International*[2] website. In some cases, though, I was unable to find the original reference and simply translated from the French version provided in the book.

I would like to thank Fred Leplat for his patient proofreading of my draft translations, Roland Wood for his work as copy editor and Duncan Chapel for seeing the whole project through on behalf of Resistance Books. I would also like to thank Andreu Coll Blackwell and Wilfried Dubois for promptly replying to my questions about the Spanish and German-language editions of the book. Thanks are also due to Michel Lequenne, who provided corrections for a handful of small errors that appeared in the original French-language edition. Finally, I would like to thank Bill Dunn and Hugo Radice for giving us permission to use their translation of the book's first chapter, which they included as a standalone piece in the collection of essays that they edited, *100 Years of Permanent Revolution: Results and Prospects* (London: Pluto Press, 2006).

Nathan Rao

---

[1] http://bit.ly/ldt
[2] http://bit.ly/etol

Foreword

The author has been a protagonist in the history of Trotskyism since 1966; this essay is therefore not meant to be a scholarly work on the subject. That would require an undertaking of an entirely different order. Rather, the more modest objective here is to shed some light and understanding on the political and theoretical controversies that have marked this turbulent history. In spite of the passage of time and the fact that I have made every effort to stand back from the subject matter, I do not claim to have entirely avoided the element of subjectivity that is inherent to personal experiences and commitments. It is a basic matter of honesty to forewarn the reader of this.

In different ways, Pierre Frank, Adolfo Gilly, Michel Lequenne, Michaël Löwy, Daniel Pereyra, Rodolphe Prager, François Sabado, Alan Thornett and Charles André Udry have contributed to this book. I am grateful to them for this.

I also want to thank Pierre Broué, Michel Dreyfus, Claude Pennetier and the team behind successive volumes of the *Maitron* dictionary of working-class and social movements. They have made an incalculable contribution to the as-yet-unwritten history of Trotskyist movements.

DANIEL BENSAÏD

Introduction:
The relevance of Trotskyism

The gaps in former French Socialist Party prime minister Lionel Jospin's memory have fed a wave of interest in "Trotskyism", whose ghostly presence now haunts the corridors of major media outlets. It has suddenly become very chic to have been "one of them" in the past. However, this temporary surge of interest has highlighted the historical and political lack of knowledge about an exotic word that brings to mind – for most of our contemporaries – the legend of the Russian revolution, the Petrograd soviet, the storming of the Winter Palace and the epic battles of the Red Army. For bibliophiles, the term is associated with the *Manifesto Towards a Free Revolutionary Art*, co-authored in 1938 by Leon Trotsky and André Breton. Film buffs remember Joseph Losey's (bad) film *The Assassination of Trotsky*, with Richard Burton in the title role and Alain Delon as the killer controlled from afar by Stalin.

Following the revelations about the prime minister's past, a number of commentators have somewhat hypocritically asserted that his ideological trajectory was not the problem. Indeed, for the brilliant student that Jospin was in the 1950s, there is nothing dishonourable about having been a "child of the Suez and Budapest" – that is to say, to have been among those who expressed solidarity simultaneously with struggles for national liberation and with the 1956 anti-bureaucratic uprisings in Poland and Hungary. On the pretext that they didn't want to bay with the pack, the "friends of the USSR" and leaders of the official Communist Parties had shut their eyes to the criminal collateral damage of the "globally positive" balance sheet of Stalinism and the blood-soaked episodes of the "Great Proletarian Cultural Revolution" in China. But Jospin's silences have also fed the fantasies and suspicions that the secretive, fractional and conspiratorial world associated with the term "entryism" has inspired over the years – stirring the wild imaginations of police and cloak-and-dagger buffs alike. Three introductory remarks to a historical understanding of Trotskyism seem to be in order:

1/ "Trotskyite" was a pejorative, stigmatizing tag invented by its adversaries. In the 1930s, at the time of the show trials, when it was midnight in the century, the Kremlin's servile brain trust even invented the oxymoron "Hitlero-Trotskyite". In the 1960s, the prolific hack of French Stalinism Léo Figuères penned a new salvo in the campaign of demonization with his made-to-order screed *Le Trotskisme, cet anti-léninisme*. The "Trotskyite" label was akin to a yellow star. For proof of this, one need only examine the long list of those whom Trotsky's companion Natalia Sedova once called "ghosts with holes in their heads": Andreu Nin, executed in the Spanish jails of the NKVD; Rudolf Klement, murdered in France; Pietro Tresso, killed by his fellow inmates from the French resistance movement; Ta Thu Thau and his comrades, assassinated by the Vietnamese Stalinists; the Greek Trotskyists executed by the special services of the Greek CP; and Zavis Kalandra, executed by the Czech Stalinists in 1950. In 1940, an assassin finally caught up to Leon Trotsky himself in Mexico. Thousands of victims of the purges and Moscow show trials were shot or disappeared into the anonymity of the Gulag. While they defiantly reappropriated a label created as an epithet, the "Trotskyites" of the 1930s preferred to define themselves as "Bolshevik Leninists", "revolutionary Marxists" and "communist internationalists" – the latter an exercise in redundancy prompted by the need to differentiate themselves from the "communism" embodied by the bureaucratic counter-revolution.

2/ Though the term Trotskyism (in the singular) refers to a common historical origin, it has come to mean so many things that it is more accurate to speak of Trotskyisms (in the plural). The various currents of "Trotskyist" origin make reference to the programmatic foundations laid down by Trotsky during the interwar period. But the scope of disagreement over the major events of the twentieth century is such that what sets these currents apart from and against one another is often as great as or greater than what unites them. When it comes to preserving a legacy, filial devotion is not always the truest measure of loyalty; there is often greater loyalty in critical disloyalty than in dogmatic sanctimoniousness. So it is more accurate to speak of *Trotskyisms* (in the plural) than of *Trotskyism* (in the singular). This is all the more true when one considers that beyond political differences there is also the specific cultural acclimatization of Anglo-American Trotskyism, of a (largely French) European Trotskyism, of Latin American Trotskyism, and even of Asian Trotskyism (in China, Vietnam, Japan and Sri Lanka). And each one of these continental groupings can be further broken down into its national specificities. A complete account would examine places where Trotskyism has established a more fragile foothold – in Africa, the Arab world and Oceania. This essay is based on personal experience; it more modestly limits itself to the major debates that have especially marked the Trotskyist movements of Europe, North America and Latin America.

3/ Lastly, many associate Trotskyism with splits and factionalism and this has provided ample fodder for sarcasm from its opponents. Yet the big organizations of the working-class – once proud of their monolithic character – are now themselves subject to the power struggles of clans, cliques and factions, in which personal rivalries often play a bigger role than programmatic disagreement. In hindsight, many of the polemics between Trotskyists can indeed appear excessive and even ridiculous. At the rational core of these debates, however, one finds a strong link to the major problems of the day. For example, the riddle of the Stalinist reaction was a key preoccupation: how was one to understand the evolution of the Russian revolution into a regime of bureaucratic terror? How was one to define – and position oneself in relation to – the unprecedented phenomenon of Stalinism? But also: how to defeat fascism and what position to take in the face of war – without getting trapped in the binary logic of contending camps or the politics of lesser evilism, which is often the shortest path to the very evil one set out to avoid. And what attitude should one have adopted to struggles for national liberation and the regimes that they engendered?

When looking at the Trotskyist quest to provide answers to these questions, it is moving to see the tremendous effort that was made to preserve some sanity in the face of the insanity and turmoil of a sombre twentieth century. However, spending such a prolonged period on the margins (Trotsky hadn't expected the movement would be in the political wilderness for so long) can create an ideal environment for all sorts of small-group pathologies. Routine swimming against the tide often gives rise to sectarianism. There was a terrible imbalance in the relationship between theoretical work and opportunities for testing theory in practice; this led to an exacerbation of doctrinal squabbles and a dogmatic fetishization of the written word. Just as there are people of the book, there is a communism of the book with an outlook that sees tactical differences as life and death questions – often wrongly, sometimes correctly. One can only know after the fact, when the owl of Minerva has spread its wings with the falling of the dusk. Forced to go against the grain of history for such a long time, Trotskyist organizations have often recruited stormy personalities, hard-nosed rebels and outsiders better suited to insubordination and dissidence than to organization-building and unity – people who Trotsky himself once described as "intelligent elements of bad character, who were never disciplined."

In spite of its best efforts, a perpetually marginalized current absorbs the very things it sets out to resist. It is worth recalling that physical violence and fear of betrayal poisoned the entire working-class movement for decades. Trotskyist organizations did not always escape the lure of aping the Bolshevik mythology concocted by Stalinism in its triumphant phase. And yet now one must guard against the illusion of political life made relatively (and provisionally) peaceful by parliamentary routine. It is true that, as Chairman Mao used to say, a revolution is not a dinner party; the interwar years during which the currents discussed in this book were formed were a time of knifings and poisonings, infiltration and provocation, liquidation and criminal violence – of the kind described in such books as Jan Valtin's *Out of the Night*, Gustav Regler's *The Owl of Minerva*, George Orwell's *Homage to Catalonia*, not to mention the many biographies and eyewitness accounts of Russia under Stalin.

Trotskyism's stormy history ultimately revolves around a single major question: how to remain "revolutionaries without revolution" (to borrow the title of surrealist André Thirion's memoirs)? As with the passionate love affairs in the novels of Marguerite Duras, it is the paradox of an imperative that is simultaneously impossible and necessary given the threats hanging over the future of humankind. Thus the heroic hand-to-hand combat with the times. In spite of a penchant for the aesthetics of defeat and moral protest, which sometimes won out over concern for immediate results, the history of Trotskyism is one of an eminently political refusal to give up, relinquish and disarm. If Trotsky and his heirs (known and unknown) are to score a posthumous victory, it will be for having deployed a wealth of courage and intelligence to stay on course – at a time when out of lassitude or opportunism so many supposedly robust figures rallied round the victors of the day, whether among the Western powers or the totalitarian bureaucracies. Having unwound their Ariadne's thread through the labyrinth of a sombre era, these rearguard fighters have rescued the vanquished from what the British historian E.P. Thompson called "the enormous condescension of posterity."

Today we see a field of ruins, with Stalinism in an advanced state of decay and Social Democracy locked in the capitalist embrace. It is a depressing scene of historical confusion, theoretical sterility and political blandness, topped off by an inability to engage with a history that won't go away. Taking all this in, we can fully appreciate the value of the victorious defeat of the Trotskyists. It has safeguarded our ability to begin again – by passing on to new generations the memory and basic understanding of the "century of extremes". This contribution will be of vital importance as they venture into the uncertainties and dangers of the century just now beginning.

1. The Baggage of Exodus

Certain "Trotskyist" theses, like the theory of permanent revolution, first appeared at the beginning of the century in relation to the Russian revolution of 1905. However, the term "Trotskyism" only appeared, as a banal term of bureaucratic jargon, in 1923-4. After the victorious civil war, and still more in 1924 after the failure of the German October and Lenin's death, the leaders of Soviet Russia and the Communist International were in an unforeseen situation of relative international stabilisation and the lasting isolation of the Soviet Union. It was no longer the social base which supported the State superstructure, but the will of the superstructure which sought to engage the base.

After his first stroke in March 1923, Lenin urged Trotsky to begin fighting Stalin on the questions of the foreign trade monopoly, nationalities, and especially the internal party regime. In a letter to the Central Committee in October 1923, Trotsky denounced the bureaucratisation of state institutions. In December of the same year, he assembled these criticisms into a series of articles calling for a New Course. This provoked the fight against "Trotskyism" and its demands: the re-establishment of internal party democracy and the adoption of an economic plan to control the uneven and centrifugal effects of the New Economic Policy. In December 1924, in Pravda, Stalin personally characterised Trotskyism as "a variety of Menshevism" and as "permanent despair". He opposed to this the daring construction of "socialism in one country", rather than waiting to be rescued by an extension of the revolution elsewhere that might never actually happen.

After the massive recruitment of the "Lenin levy" in 1924, the few thousand veterans of October no longer weighed very heavily in the party's membership relative to the hundreds of thousands of newcomers, amongst whom were many last-minute careerists. In a country lacking of democratic traditions and following the slaughter of the Great War, the hardships of the civil war left a people accustomed to extreme forms of social and physical violence. The upheavals of war and civil war led to a "great leap backwards" and a reversion to an archaic level of development compared to that reached before 1914. Of the 4 million inhabitants of Petrograd in

1917, there remained no more than about 1.7 million in 1929. More than 380,000 workers left production and only 80,000 remained at work. The workers citadel, the Putilov works, lost four-fifths of its employees, while more than thirty million peasants experienced food shortage and famine. The devastated cities lived on the back of authoritarian campaigns of requisition. "In truth," notes the historian Moshe Lewin, "the State was formed on the basis of regressive social development."

Privilege thrives on scarcity: therein lie the fundamental roots of bureaucratisation. In a journal dictated in 1923 to his secretaries, Lenin, already sick, deemed that "we call 'ours' an apparatus which is deeply foreign to us and which represents a hotchpotch of middle-class survivals and tsarists". That year, the prices of manufactures had practically tripled compared to pre-1914 levels, whereas farm prices had increased by less than 50 %. This disproportion explains the imbalance between city and countryside, and the refusal of the peasants to deliver their harvests at imposed low prices while there was nothing to buy.

The Bolshevik leaders had always conceived the revolution in Russia as the first step towards a European revolution or, at least, as a prelude to German revolution. The question put in 1923 was therefore: how to hold on until a possible resumption of the revolutionary movement in Europe? In 1917, all the Russian parties admitted that the country was not ripe for socialism. However, the "democrat" Miliukov himself estimated that it was no more ready for democracy. He saw no alternative between the military dictatorship of Kornilov and that of the Soviets. This meant a pitiless fight between revolution and counter-revolution.

From before Lenin's death, responses diverged. The strategy of "construction of socialism in one country", defended by Stalin and his allies, subordinated the chances of world revolution to the interests of the Soviet bureaucracy; that of "the permanent revolution", developed by Trotsky and the Left Opposition, subordinated the future of the Russian revolution to the extension of the world revolution. These strategies implied divergent answers in relation to the principal international events: Anglo-Russian relations in 1926, the second Chinese revolution of 1927, the rise of Nazism in Germany, and later the radically contrary attitudes towards the Spanish civil war, the German-Soviet pact of 1939 and preparations for war.

The two strategies were equally opposed on the Soviet Union's policies at home. Trotsky and the Left Opposition proposed after 1924 a "new course" aimed at reviving Soviet democracy and the role of the Party. They put forward policies of planning and industrialisation aimed at reducing the tensions between agriculture and industry. However, they came to oppose Stalin's brutal about-turn of 1928 from Bukharin's "socialism at a snail"s pace' to forced collectivization and the accelerated industrialisation of the First Five-Year Plan, which denuded the countryside and led to the great famine of 1932 in the Ukraine.

Faced with such clear alternatives, some historians have wondered about Trotsky's relative passivity immediately after Lenin's death, his reluctance to start a ruthless fight against Stalin, his agreeing to sweep Lenin's testament under the carpet. Self-interest provides plausible and logical, explanations. He was, in the mid-twenties, perfectly conscious of the brittleness of a revolution whose working-class and urban base was thin, and of the need to work with a backward peasantry which constituted the overwhelming majority of the population. Given such an unstable equilibrium, favourable to authoritarian Bonapartist solutions, he refused to be pushed by the army (where his popularity remained high) and by the officer caste, because a military coup d'état would only have accelerated the process of bureaucratisation.

However, the political struggle had in fact been joined from 1923. By 1926, a united opposition was established which saw itself as a tendency that respected the legal authority of the Party; their perspective was one of redirecting and reforming the regime. In May 1927, after the defeat of the second Chinese revolution, they called for a militant mass mobilisation. In October of the same year, on the tenth birthday of the revolution, Zinoviev and Trotsky were excluded from the party. The latter was exiled to Alma Ata, while more than 1,500 oppositionists were deported. The purges began.

In 1929, faced with a catastrophic economic situation, Stalin turned against the right of the party. He seemed, by instituting the first five-year plan, to be adopting certain suggestions of the opposition. This turn precipitated a split among the Opposition. Some of its most prestigious leaders saw in this "revolution from above" a swing to the left. Capitulations and defections followed one after another. For Trotsky, those reconciled with the Thermidorean regime were from now on "lost souls": planning without the restoration of socialist democracy would only further reinforce the power of the bureaucracy. Thus began a long exodus, forced to the margins of the mass movement.

These tragic inter-war struggles shaped the original defining characteristics of Trotskyism. Its essence can be summarised in four points.

1. The opposition of the theory of permanent revolution to that of "socialism in one country".

The elements of this strategy had emerged from the earlier Russian revolution of 1905. They were elaborated during the 1920s and found their full expression in Trotsky's theses on the second Chinese revolution of 1927:

"With regard to countries with a belated bourgeois development, especially the colonial and semi-colonial countries, the theory of the permanent revolution signifies that the complete and genuine solution of their tasks of achieving democracy and national emancipation is conceivable only through the dictatorship of the proletariat as the leader of the subjugated nation, above all of its peasant masses.... The conquest of power by the proletariat does not complete the revolution, but only opens it. Socialist construction is conceivable only on the foundation of the class struggle, on a national and international scale.... The completion of the socialist revolution within national limits is unthinkable. One of the basic reasons for the crisis in bourgeois society is the fact that the productive forces created by it can no longer be reconciled with the framework of the national state. From this follow...imperialist wars.... Different countries will go through this process at different tempos. Backward countries may, under certain conditions, arrive at the dictatorship of the proletariat sooner than advanced countries, but they will come later than the latter to socialism" (Trotsky 1928/1962, pp.152-155).

In his introduction to the 1930 German edition of his texts on Permanent Revolution, Trotsky denounces the Stalinist amalgam of *"messianic nationalism ... supplemented by bureaucratically abstract internationalism"* (ibid., p.25). He maintains that the socialist revolution remains, even after the seizure of power, *"a continual internal struggle"* through which society *"continues to change its complexion"*, and within which inevitable shocks arise from *"the various groupings within this society in transformation"*. This theory is imbued with a nonlinear and non-mechanical conception of history, where the law of 'combined and uneven development' determines only a range of possibilities whose outcome is not determined in advance. *"Marxism"*, writes Trotsky, *"takes its point of departure from world economy, not as a sum of national parts but as a mighty and independent reality which has been created by the international division of labour and the world market, and which in our epoch imperiously dominates the national markets"* (ibid., p.22)

2. On transitional demands, the United Front and the fight against Fascism.

The questions put in the light of the Russian revolution were: how to mobilise the greatest possible numbers; how to raise the level of consciousness through action; and how to create the most effective alliance of forces for the inescapable confrontation with the ruling classes. This is what the Bolsheviks had known how to do in 1917 around the vital questions of bread, peace, land. It was a question of moving beyond abstract discussion of the intrinsic virtue of the claims, whether reformist by nature (because compatible with the established order) or revolutionary by nature (because incompatible with this order). The appropriateness of the demands depends on their mobilising value in connection with a concrete situation, and on their educational value for those who enter into struggle. The concept of 'transitional demands' overcomes sterile antinomies between a reformist gradualism which believes in changing society without revolutionising it, and a fetishism of the 'glorious day' which reduces revolution to its climactic moment, to the detriment of the patient work of organisation and education.

This debate is directly related to the one at the centre of strategic discussions on the program of the Fifth and the Sixth Congresses of the Communist International. Reporting on the question in 1925, Bukharin reaffirmed the validity of 'the tactics of the offensive' of the beginning of the 1920s. On the other hand, at the Fifth Congress, the German representative Thalheimer supported the idea of the united front and transitional demands. He argued in particular:

"One only has to look at the history of the Second International and its disintegration to recognise that it is precisely the separation between day-to-day questions and broad objectives which constituted the starting point of its descent into opportunism [...] The specific difference between us and the reformist socialists lies not in the fact that we want to eliminate from our program demands for reform, by whatever name we give them, in order to distance ourselves from them. Rather, it consists in the fact that we locate these transitional demands in the closest relationship to our principles and our aims".

The question was again on the agenda of the Sixth Congress of 1928, under profoundly different conditions. Exiled in Turkey since 1929, Trotsky benefited from his enforced retreat to assess more deeply the previous ten years of revolutionary experiences. This reflection provided the material for the texts on *The Communist*

International after Lenin. In his critique of the program of the CI, published in Constantinople in 1929, Trotsky condemned the abandonment of the slogan of the Socialist United States of Europe. He rejected any confusion between his theory of permanent revolution and Bukharin's theory of the permanent offensive. He again characterised fascism as a 'state of civil war' carried out by capitalism against the proletariat.

Immediately after the Congress, through an about turn which ran in parallel with the policy of liquidation of the kulaks and forced collectivisation in Soviet Union, the CI adopted an orientation of 'class against class'. This made social democracy the principal enemy and produced a fatal division in the German labour movement faced with the rise of the Nazism. In a booklet entitled The Third Period of Error of the Communist International, Trotsky denounced this disastrous course not as a relapse into revolutionary enthusiasm, explicable as youthful leftism, but as a senile and bureaucratic leftism subordinated to the interests of the Kremlin and the zigzags of its diplomacy. In his *History of the Russian Revolution*, he insisted on the serious study of indices of mass radicalisation (the evolution of trade-union power, electoral results, the strike rate) instead of abstractedly proclaiming the constant possibility of revolutionary action: *"the activity of the masses can take very different forms according to conditions. At certain times, the masses can be completely absorbed by economic struggles and express very little interest in political questions. Alternatively, after having undergone several important reverses on the economic front, they can abruptly shift attention onto the political field."* His *Writings on Germany* day-by-day advance proposals for united action to overcome the resistible rise of Nazism. They provide a brilliant example of concrete political thought adjusted to the changes in the economic situation. They were thunderbolts hurled at German Communist Party 'orthodoxy', which was wedded to the stupid prophecy according to which 'after Hitler, comes the turn of Thälmann [then Secretary-General of the German CP]'.

In 1938, the founding Program of the Fourth International (or Transitional Program) summarised the lessons of these experiences:

"In the process of their daily struggle the masses should be helped to find a bridge between their immediate demands and the program of the socialist revolution. This bridge must consist of a system of transitional demands, based on current conditions and the real consciousness of broad layers of the working class, and inexorably leading them towards the single conclusion: the conquest of power by the proletariat [...] The Fourth International

does not reject the claims of the old minimum program insofar as they retain some vitality. It tirelessly defends workers' democratic rights and their social achievements. But it undertakes this daily work from the revolutionary point of view."

The program included demands for sliding scales of wages and hours, for workers control of production (a school for the planned economy) and financial transparency, for "the expropriation of certain groups of capitalists", for the nationalisation of credit. It attached particular importance to democratic and national claims in the colonial and semi-colonial countries. This program did not constitute a ready-made model of society; rather it developed a way of understanding action in which the emancipation of the workers remained the task of workers themselves.

3. The fight against Stalinism and the bureaucracy.

At the beginning of the 1920s, certain Soviet economists saw the world capitalist economy plunging into endless stagnation. Trotsky was one of the first to analyse its relative revival. In this context, he came to think of the Soviet economy not as a socialist economy, but as an 'economy in transition' in a country subjected to constant military threats and forced to devote a disproportionate share of its meagre resources to defence. It was thus not a question of building an ideal society in one country, but of gaining time, while awaiting the ebb and flow of the world revolution on whose final authority the future of the Russian revolution depended. The Russian revolution would remain constrained by the world market, and by competition with countries with more developed technology and higher labour productivity, for as a long as it remained unsupported by the revolutionary movement of more developed countries.

Within the framework of these contradictions, Trotsky was one of the first to perceive the danger of the bureaucracy as a new social force enjoying social privileges related to its monopoly of political power. If, at the time of the civil war and War Communism, he had been in favour of authoritarian methods, as testified by his worst book, *Terrorism and Communism* (1921), since 1923 he had started to analyse bureaucratisation as a social phenomenon, even if in his eyes the 'new middle-class' of the kulaks and Nepmen still remained the principal danger. This decisive question of the periodisation of the bureaucratic counter-revolution continued to confront the Russian and international revolutionary movements. It was a question of knowing if the 'Soviet Thermidor' was already achieved or yet to come.

The bureaucratic counter-revolution was not a single event, symmetrical to that of October, but a drawn-out, cumulative process of different levels and stages. From October 1917 to the Stalinist Gulag, there is no simple continuity, but different levels of repression by and weight of the bureaucracy. At the same time as forced collectivisation, a crucial reform of the detention system came into effect in June 1929, generalising work camps for all condemned prisoners with more than three-year sentences. Confronted by the great famines of 1932-1933 and the importance of internal migrations, a decision of December 1932 introduced internal passports. The law of December 1st 1934 introduced procedures that provided the legal instruments of the great terror. Then began the genuinely terrorist cycle marked by the great purges of 1936-1938. More half the delegates to the congress of 1934 were eliminated; more than 30,000 cadres from an army of 178 000 were killed. In parallel, the bureaucratic state apparatus exploded: according to the statistics of Moshe Lewin, the numbers of administrative staff went from 1,450,000 in 1928 to 7,500,000 in 1939, while the number of white collar workers leaped from 4 million to nearly 14 million. The state apparatus devoured the party, which thought it had the power to control it.

Under the bureaucratic knout, the country thus witnessed an upheaval without equivalent in the world. Between 1926 and 1939, the cities grew by 30 million inhabitants, and their paid labour force went from 10 to 22 million. It resulted in a massive ruralisation of the cities and the despotic imposition of new work discipline. This transformation by forced march was accompanied by the exaltation of nationalism and a massive rise in careerism. In this great social and geographical whirl, as Moshe Lewin comments ironically, society was in a certain sense 'classless', because all classes were formless, in perpetual fusion.

Despite the differences in their outlooks, authors as different as Trotsky and Hannah Arendt agree that the first Five-Year Plan and the great purges of the 1930s were the qualititative turning-point after which it became possible to speak about bureaucratic counter-revolution (for Trotsky) or totalitarianism (for Arendt). Trotsky's contribution was to provide the elements of a materialist understanding of the bureaucratic counter-revolution, where social and historical conditions take precedence over palace intrigues or the psychology of the actors. He does not reduce colossal events involving multitudes to the whims of a 'history from above', made by supreme guides or great helmsmen. His contribution therefore does not end the debate, and definitely does not solve the historical problems which continued to divide his 'orthodox' and 'heterodox' heirs.

He particularly sought to locate the stages of the process by which the bureaucracy became autonomous and power became concentrated in the hands of one individual. The extent of crystallisation of privileges, the relationship between classes, Party and State, and the bureaucratic orientation of international politics represent various indicators which he combined to try to determine these stages. The most telling element of this reactionary break, however, was not sociological, but political: it lay in the bankruptcy of the Communist International in relation to the rise and victory of Nazism in Germany. In 1937, when the Moscow trials and the great terror were in full swing, Trotsky corrected his vision: *"We had formerly defined Stalinism as a bureaucratic centrism. This assertion is now redundant. The interests of the Bonapartist bureaucracy no longer correspond to the hybrid character of centrism. The counter-revolutionary character of Stalinism on the world arena is definitively established".* From this followed the need to give up the position of realignment and reform of the USSR: *"the central task from now on becomes that of overthrowing the Thermidorian bureaucracy itself".* This revolution qualifies as political insofar as it is supposed to be based on existing social rights (state property and planning). In his essay on Trotsky, Ernest Mandel uses the paradoxical formula for Stalinism of *"political counter-revolution in the revolution".* Such ambiguous formula led to an insistence on characterising the state as a bureaucratically-degenerated workers state, thus attributing to it a social content that gave rise to many ambiguities.

The program of the political revolution still included a series of democratic claims already advanced in 1927 in the Platform of the Left Opposition: *"1) To prevent any attempt to lengthen the working day; 2) To increase wages, at least in relation to current industrial output; 5) To reduce rents for ...".* This platform categorically condemned the practice of removing elected trade-union representatives under the pretext of internal party dissent. It advocated full independence for factory committees and local committees with respect to the state administration. On the other hand, it did not call into question *"the position as a single party occupied by the Communist Party of Soviet Union".* It was satisfied to announce that this situation, *"absolutely essential to the revolution",* generated a series of *"particular dangers".* The *Transitional Program* of 1938 marks a fundamental change on this point. There, political pluralism, the independence of the trade unions from the Party and the state and democratic freedoms become questions of principle, insofar as they express the heterogeneity of the proletariat and the conflicts of interests likely within it that are likely to persist well beyond the conquest of power. In *The Revolution Betrayed*, Trotsky had shown the theoretical bases of this principled pluralism. Classes are not homogeneous *"as if the conscience of a class corresponded exactly to its place in society"*. They are *"torn by internal antagonisms and arrive at their ultimate goals only through competing tendencies, alignments and parties. One can recognise with some reservations which party is a fraction of which class, but as a class is made of a number of fractions the same class can form several parties"*. Thus the proletariat of the Soviet society *"is not less, but much more heterogeneous and complex that that of the capitalist country, and it can consequently provide a largely sufficient breeding ground for the formation of several parties"* Trotsky concluded from this that the democratisation of the Soviets was from now on *"inconceivable without the right to the multi-party system"*.

4. The question of the Party and the International.

This is the fourth great question constitutive of original 'Trotskyism'. It is the organisational corollary of the theory of the permanent revolution, and of understanding the revolution as an international process. Trotsky's last fight for a new International, which he regarded as the most important of his life, was against the nationalist evolution of the Soviet regime and its foreseeable consequence: the liquidation of the Communist International itself, made official in 1943.

2. Trotsky's final struggle

The 1930s saw a huge number of major developments: Hitler's arrival in power in 1933; the crushing of the Vienna insurrection in 1934; the Civil War in Spain and the Popular Front in France; Mao Zedong's Long March and the establishment of the Yenan Republic; the Trials and the Great Terror in the Soviet Union; Munich and the German-Soviet Pact; the *Anschluss* and the carving up of Poland. This cascading series of events read like the chronicle of a war foretold. It was therefore urgent to preserve and hand down the movement's heritage. The handful of internationalists opposed to the *Union sacrée* (patriotic "sacred union") of 1914 had lacked an organizational framework; it was therefore also necessary that such a body be created as the new war grew closer.

In 1929, Trotsky was still denying that he wanted to build a new International. "This idea is completely wrong." This denial reflected his profound conviction that the counter-revolution in the USSR had not yet been completed. He took the example of the Second International, whose turn to class collaboration did not suddenly occur when it voted in support of war credits. Well before 1914, there had been ample signs of the degeneration of the Second International. They had been as much on the level of theory (with the controversy on revisionism at the beginning of the century involving Bernstein, Kautsky and Rosa Luxemburg) as on the level of politics (with the adoption of chauvinist positions on the colonial question and the parliamentarist drift of French socialism under Millerand) and the signs of bureaucratization decried by Georges Sorel, Roberto Michels and Antonio Labriola. But this had not been enough to demonstrate outright failure. In order to conclude that a new International was needed, it took the crucial test of 4 August 1914, when Socialists supported the *Union sacrée*.

So long as he held to the idea of an incomplete Thermidor in the Soviet Union, Trotsky argued for the "reconstruction" of the International and the Communist Party of the Soviet Union. In 1932, he still defined the Left Opposition as "a faction of International communism." Nonetheless, he was already contemplating the events that could lead to a change in his position: "A disaster such as the fall of the Soviet state would without a doubt also bring about the fall of the Third International. Similarly, the victory of fascism in Germany and the crushing of the German proletariat would make it very difficult for the Comintern to survive the consequences of its disastrous policy." One year later, the latter event came to pass with Hitler and the Nazis' accession to power. Trotsky's verdict was immediate: "The German proletariat will rise again, the German Communist Party never!"

Despite all these events, the fate of the Communist International had not in fact been sealed. The young Communist Parties had not all simultaneously become simple appendages of the Soviet bureaucracy. The Stalinization of the International was uneven. In some countries, such as Spain, it nipped the nascent communist movement in the bud. In others, such as Sweden, but also in Germany and Catalonia, it led to breaks and splits. Finally, in others, the subordination of Communist Parties to the interests of the Kremlin bureaucracy became the object of huge struggles all through the 1930s. As the historian Isaac Deutscher has pointed out, the degeneration of the Third International was different from, and more difficult to understand than that of the Second International, which had been slowly corrupted by its progressive integration into state institutions, by the securing of parliamentary positions, and by the social advancement of the trade-union bureaucracies. Those who became Communists at the beginning of the 1930s, on the other hand, were more likely to face victimization at the workplace and police repression than they were to be showered with perks. In the eyes of party activists, the Stalinist reaction often appeared to be a kind of "bureaucratic heroism" – very different from the institutional comfort served up to the trained seals of Social Democracy.

Following four months of reflection, Trotsky duly noted the absence of any change in course by the Third International and called for a new International. This decision was not based on a forecast of any sort but on the crucial experience of what had occurred; not on subjective impressions but on actual upheavals; not on predictions but on facts. In 1930, he had written, "It is clear that all the possibilities and probabilities of an evolution towards Bonapartism diminish the likelihood of success of the path of reforms [in the Soviet Union], but the effects cannot be measured in advance. We remain on the path of reform." On 23 July 1933, he persisted, "Even though a number of us have been convinced for some time that the Communist International was destined to failure, it was impossible for us to proclaim a new International ourselves. We have always raised this question in relation to great historical events that would bring about a historical examination of the Stalinized Comintern."

Of course, it is no easy matter to determine the exact moment at which the historical fork in the road occurs. The very act of choosing a decisive event brings with it an unavoidable element of subjectivity. Indeed, one can wonder if the fate of the Communist International had not already been sealed in 1927 with the tragedy of the second Chinese Revolution described in André Malraux's novel *Man's Fate*, or in 1930 with the brutality of the forced collectivization and the first round of purges in the Soviet Union. Trotsky suggested that these questions were better left to historians. The Nazi arrival in power changed Europe's fate and clearly represented a crucial turning point in the interwar period.

But the hesitation to declare the need for a new orientation stems from an additional problem. It was not merely a matter, as in 1914, of reading out the funeral oration of a defunct International – but also of dealing with the unprecedented problems raised by the transformation of the Soviet Union. Did the call for the formation of a new international revolutionary party, including in the Soviet Union, not imply calling for a new revolution in the Soviet Union itself? According to Jan Van Heijenoort, who was his secretary during the 1930s, Trotsky began to consider this prospect between March and July 1933 but only embraced it in 1936. Given the consequences of such a decision, the time spent examining the matter does not seem excessive, but quite reasonable.

The decision to build a new international organization was based first and foremost on a programmatic judgement. On what basis should it take place? Though references to the Communist Manifesto and the first four congresses of the Communist International provide necessary guidance, even the latter was no longer sufficient. In the space of ten years, the international class struggle had given rise to events requiring new demarcations: the bureaucratic counter-revolution in the Soviet Union; the victory of fascism in Italy and Germany; and the lessons of the second Chinese Revolution. Far from being an inviolable tablet of Holy Scriptures, the program is constantly enriched by new foundational experiences. The lessons drawn since October 1917 were summarized in a short 1933 document known as the *Eleven Points of the Left Opposition*. It concisely set forth the essential points of analysis:

- 1.The intransigent defence of the independence of working-class parties. This was the lesson drawn from the fatal subordination of the Chinese Communist Party to Chiang Kai-shek's nationalist Kuomintang.

- 2. Countering the theory of socialism in one country with the theory of permanent revolution and re-affirming the international character of the proletarian revolution against globalized capitalism.
- 3. Characterizing the Soviet Union as a "bureaucratically degenerated workers state", and therefore defending it against imperialism and any attempt at capitalist restoration.
- 4. A condemnation of Stalin's economic policy and of the tragic adventure of "forced collectivization".
- 5. The need to work in mass trade unions, against the sectarian policy of trade-union splits promoted by the Comintern during the "Third Period".
- 6. Rejection of the concept of the "democratic dictatorship of the proletariat and peasantry" understood by Comintern leaders as an historical stage distinct from the dictatorship of the proletariat.
- 7. The need to mobilize the masses around transitional demands – for example around democratic slogans in the colonial countries and under dictatorial regimes. This point settled the debate on program that had taken place at the 5th and 6th congresses of the Communist International.
- 8. The need for the policy of a united front of the working class, as much against collaboration with bourgeois parties as against the disastrous sectarianism of the "Third Period of the Comintern's errors."
- 9. The categorical condemnation of the supposed theory of "social-fascism" which likens social-democratic parties to fascist parties and no longer makes any distinction between parliamentary democracy and fascist dictatorship.
- 10. And the need for democratic functioning within the party to counter the bureaucratic degeneration of both the Communist Party of the Soviet Union and the Communist International.
- A point added in July of the same year further proclaims the "need to create an authentic Communist International capable of applying the above principles." Five years later, the *Transitional Program* added the call for a new political revolution (an "insurrectionary upheaval") in the Soviet Union, for the "downfall of the Thermidorian bureaucracy",

for the "regeneration and development of soviet democracy", for the "legalization of soviet democracy", for returning to factory committees the right to control production, for an end to secret diplomacy, and for a public review of all political trials.

The year 1934 saw a number of new and important political developments. In February, the Schutzbund insurrection in Vienna was crushed and there were fascist demonstrations in Paris. Aware of the threat the rise of fascism posed to the very existence of Social Democracy, Trotsky concluded that left currents would inevitably arise within its parties. A few months later, the participation of Spanish Socialists in the Asturias insurrection confirmed this forecast. Trotsky drew practical conclusions for Spain, Belgium and France. He argued that the small forces of the Left Opposition should take their place within the united front against fascism by joining the Social Democratic parties. Known as the "French turn", this orientation immediately gave rise to debates and division. It was the first instance of what would become known as "entryism", often cited as an example of the manoeuvring practises employed by Trotskyist organizations.

Following the signing of the Soviet-French pact in May 1935, the Seventh Congress of the Communist International endorsed a new line advocating Popular Fronts. This created yet another new state of affairs. This U-turn by the Stalinist parties set the stage for the bureaucratic unity of party apparatuses, forging agreement with each other at the expense of revolutionary currents. This led in short order to the expulsion of the "Bolshevik-Leninist" current from the French Socialist Party. It was necessary to change course anew, making the building of independent organizations a priority yet again.

Trotsky also proposed the accelerated construction and proclamation of the Fourth International, refusing to continue playing for time in anticipation of hypothetical reinforcements. Still, the fight for a new International encountered new difficulties at the end of 1935. The French and American sections were divided on the question of entryism. And in Moscow, the series of political show trials were just beginning. "The wind now blows against us," Trotsky observed. Expecting that the dialectic of defeats would lead straight to war, he felt there was no more time to lose. In July 1936, the Conference of the "Movement for the Fourth International" brought together organizations from nine countries. Some twenty other groups were unable to send delegates. But for some obscure reason, the Conference held off on proclaiming the Fourth International.

- It was only in September 1938 – after the big Stalinist purges in the USSR and following complete defeat in Spain and France – that the Founding Conference of the Fourth International finally took place. It adopted the document known as the *Transitional Program* alongside statutes defining the new International as the "world party of the socialist revolution." Only three delegates spoke out against this decision, with the Pole Hersch Mendel-Sztokfisz as their main spokesperson. He reminded delegates that Marx, Engels and Lenin had been careful not to found the First, Second or Third International in periods of retreat; they had waited for a vigorous revival of struggles before forging ahead. In 1938, though, there was no mass party on which to base the new International. Proclaiming an International in such conditions, he warned, ran the risk of producing a sterile groupuscule that would discredit the very idea for a long time to come.

Trotsky was well aware that the conditions in which the Fourth International was being created were extremely difficult and entirely without precedent. It would be a minority International, with no mass sections. He described it as an "International of cadres" whose main task was to preserve a heritage and prepare for the future. It was born out of a series of defeats for the world proletariat, of which the bureaucratic counter-revolution in the USSR was not the least severe. It was founded in a context in which the working-class movement, far from being at an early stage of development and experience, was tightly organized in a number of key countries by Social Democratic and Stalinist apparatuses mutually strengthening each other. And the international Stalinist current had a specific material base at its disposal – thanks to the existence of a "socialist fatherland", however "bureaucratically degenerated".

In such conditions, "a straight line is scarcely feasible." It would be necessary to find a strong foothold in order to go from this minority International to the building of a new mass International. Trotsky wrote to the left Socialist Marceau Pivert, "The Bolshevik-Leninists see themselves as a faction of the International that is being built. They are prepared to work hand in hand with other truly revolutionary factions."

These trials and tribulations of the period encompassing the formation of the Fourth International raise a number of questions:

1. Trotsky's prescriptions during the 1930s cleave very closely to the ups and downs of a rapidly changing situation. Taking just the French case as an example, between 1932 and 1939 there were no

fewer than five tactical turns. In 1932, the policy was to remain inside the Communist Party in order to build a Left opposition with a view to the reconstruction of the Communist International. In 1933, it was about establishing an independent organization. In 1934, it meant entering the Socialist Party in anticipation of the appearance of Left currents within its ranks. In 1935, the tactic was to leave the Socialists to build an independent organization against the bureaucratic unity of the Social Democratic and Stalinist apparatuses. And in 1939, he advocated joining Marceau Pivert's Workers and Peasants Socialist Party (PSOP) after its break from Social Democracy. This political flexibility is the polar opposite of the rigid dogmatism that some attribute to Trotsky. Organizationally, however, this entailed an intelligent but destructive juggling act involving sharp turns, each of which created division and often led to splits. In this way, losses cancelled out the gains that had been made.

2. In keeping with arguments similar to those advanced by delegates opposed to the proclamation of the new International in 1938, the creation of the Fourth International has often been judged to have been premature. Trotsky thought it probable that the Kremlin bureaucracy would not survive the test of the war and that the war itself would open up a period of revolutionary upheavals and political realignments comparable to what had been seen in the wake of the First World War. However, it is incorrect to say that the Fourth International was founded on the basis of this forecast. On the contrary, the need to lay the foundations for a new International flowed from the relationship of class forces on a global scale, the tasks dictated by the world situation and the crisis of the leadership of the workers movement on the eve of the war. One can challenge this course of action, but understanding its internal logic is another matter. The need for an International – even a minority one – to confront the chauvinist degeneration of the major working-class organizations was not based on an inspired piece of prognostication. Rather, for Trotsky, this course of action was essential in order to prepare for the different possible outcomes of the war.

Trotsky's writings from these formative years in the history of the Fourth International are shot through with impatience and harshness towards close associates such as Andreu Nin and Victor Serge. These excessive polemics sometimes set the tone for subsequent debates and fuelled the tendency of Trotskyist movements to tear themselves apart over baseless accusations. While not justifying the excesses of these years, a number of explanations can help us to understand them.

- The exasperation is on a par with the seriousness of the stakes involved during this period. From one defeat to the next, the march to war was becoming unavoidable. Trotsky foresaw the dangers of fascism in Europe; he was aware of the scale of the bureaucratic reaction in the Soviet Union; and he understood that the coming conflict would be even worse for humankind than the 1914-1918 war. The alternative between "socialism or barbarism" was no longer a distant historical matter but rather an immediate choice. In spite of confident proclamations about the future of humanity, despair pierces through his writings after each missed opportunity and in the face of the downward spiral of defeats.

- This political battle was being waged at the same time as Trotsky's personal tragedies were mounting and becoming intertwined with the great historical tragedy playing itself out on the wider stage. Trotsky had not heard from his son Sergei Sedov and his son-in-law Platon Volkov, who had gone missing during the Purges. His daughter Zina had committed suicide in Germany in 1933. His eldest son and closest collaborator, Leon Sedov, died in Paris in 1938 in controversial circumstances. There were countless disappearances and assassinations amongst his supporters: Ignace Reiss in Switzerland, Rudolf Klement in Paris, Andreu Nin in Alcalá de Henares (near Madrid) and Christian Rakovsky in Russia. Condemned to wander across a "planet without a visa", he had himself been exiled to Alma Ata and then deported to Prinkipo (Turkey); he then spent two years in France and several gloomy months in Norway before leaving for Mexico, where he arrived in February 1937. Having barely alighted from the boat, and looking forward to a new start in a new country, the past caught up with Trotsky and his companion Natalia when they received news of the Second Moscow Trial. "The totalitarian apparatus poisoned the accused with lies before crushing them." This was the perfected destruction of every fibre of the soul, "a trial of automatons, not of human beings," Trotsky said at the time – a theatre of shadows in which "the accused no longer exists as a person."

- The struggle against the lies of the Moscow Trials and against Stalin's crimes was not just a gallant last stand for the history books. In his memoirs, the head of the Red Orchestra Leopold Trepper paid tribute to this struggle:

"The Trotskyists were the only ones who wouldn't confess."
Between October 1936 and March 1937, they organized a
132-day hunger strike demanding an eight-hour workday,
the elimination of rations geared to output, the separation of
political prisoners and common law criminals, and the self-
organization of prisoners. To resist the totalitarian machine,
one required not only strength of character but also a
thorough understanding of this illogical moment of human
history alongside unfailing political conviction.

- Thus the importance for Trotsky of holding a commission of
  inquiry, where he pledged to open up his archives and
  demolish point by point the legal masquerade of the
  Moscow prosecutors. Called upon to participate in this
  commission of inquiry, a number of intellectuals declined to
  do so – invoking the casuistic pretext that it is impossible to
  prove a negative. However, believing that it was a matter of
  "fundamental principles of truth and justice," the
  philosopher and logician John Dewey agreed to chair the
  commission. "I accepted the responsibilities of this position
  because I realized that to act otherwise would be a betrayal
  of my life's work." Dewey was fascinated by this exile who
  had presided over the Soviets and led the Red Army, and
  was now virtually alone at the head of a tiny International
  and its miniature parties. There is in Trotsky, Dewey wrote,
  "that certain quality of incompleteness that misfortune adds
  to virtue."

Running through Trotsky's closely argued presentation of the
facts before the Commission is an engaging reflection on history.
"Until today, mankind has not succeeded in rationalizing its history.
That is a fact. We human beings have not succeeded in rationalizing
our bodies and minds. True, psychoanalysis tries to teach us to
harmonize our body and mentality, but until today without great
success. But the question is not if we can reach the absolute
perfection of society. The question is, for me, whether we can make
great steps forward. Not to rationalize the character of our history,
because after every great step forward mankind makes a small
detour, even a great step backward. I regret it very much, but I am
not responsible for it. (Laughter) After the revolution, after the
world revolution, it is possible that mankind will become tired. For
some, a part of them, a new religion can arise, and so on. But I am
sure that in general it would be a very great step forward." In
Trotsky's eyes, this solitary battle in an out-of-the-way garden in a
suburb of Mexico City was perhaps the most important one. October

could have taken place without him, and perhaps even without Lenin. When history is going in the right direction, it finds the people it needs. It is in defeat that one becomes irreplaceable. When adverse winds are blowing, good men and women are hard to find.

Appearing before the Dewey Commission[3], the task at hand was nothing more and nothing less than exposing the lies before history could become shrouded in myth. The Commission released its findings in December 1937, supported by a case file 600-pages thick. "[...] Point 21: We find that the Prosecutor fantastically falsified Trotsky's role before, during and after the October Revolution [...] Point 23: We therefore find Trotsky and Sedov not guilty." On learning the news, Trotsky cried out, "Two lines! But two lines that will weigh heavily in the annals of humankind." Indeed, since that time, archival research has amply confirmed the Commission's findings.

3. A heritage with no instruction manual

The fight for the Fourth International bridged the gap between two historical periods and two generations of political activists. It was thoroughly bound up with the political view one had of the coming war. War is an extreme experience; it is the acid test *par excellence*. It mercilessly reveals the true face of policies, organizations and people's characters. It is a watershed event.

By 1937, Trotsky believed that war was probable within two years. He predicted that Hitlerite Germany would begin to make major gains in the West without winning total victory over England. He forecast that France would be divided up, overrun and relegated to the rank of second-rate power. Following Munich, he denounced the rotten compromise as incapable of preserving the peace; and he foresaw the possibility of collusion between Hitler and Stalin. Following the German-Soviet Pact of August 1939, which plunged many Communist activists into disarray, he repeatedly condemned Stalin's economic assistance to Hitler. In spite of his fierce struggle against the Kremlin bureaucracy, he continued to describe himself as an unconditional defender of Soviet Russia and its social relations

---

[3] See 'The case of Leon Trotsky' http://bit.ly/CaseofLT

based on state-owned property. Shortly before his death, he considered American entry into the war unavoidable. For Trotsky, the real issue in the war was competition between Germany and the USA for world leadership at the expense of Britain.

Trotsky would be assassinated in August 1940 and therefore knew nothing of the extermination camps, the final solution, the recourse to nuclear weapons, or the birth of the new world order at Yalta and Potsdam. His last writings nevertheless provide an unfinished contribution to the debates between his heirs, in which questions about the war and the characterization of the Soviet Union were inextricably intertwined. In contemporary societies, class struggle provides a thread of intelligibility to events which at first glance appear to be a senseless tangle of noise and fury, passions and madness. But history cannot be reduced to a simple confrontation with clear-cut frontlines; it is refracted through the mediation of states, nations and territories. The task is to work one's way through all this complexity. In his analysis of the Second World War, the Belgian leader of the Fourth International Ernest Mandel spoke of the interlacing of an inter-imperialist war (between the United States, Germany and Japan), a defensive war waged by a state born out of revolution (the Soviet Union against Germany), wars of national liberation (China against Japan), wars of resistance against foreign occupation (France, Yugoslavia, Greece), and civil wars (Greece, Italy, China). In this labyrinth, frontlines overlapped and cut across each other. The small groupings of supporters of the Fourth International – which had been in existence for only two years – found it very difficult to orient themselves in this complex situation. Communication was very difficult and a number of experienced members had quite simply been liquidated by both fascist and Stalinist repression. It is possible to avoid the "enormous condescension of posterity" while maintaining a critical eye, so long as one seeks to understand before casting judgement.

The Emergency Conference

Germany's lightning attack on Poland began within a few days of the dramatic signing of the German-Soviet Pact in late August 1939. Stalin, in turn, asserted his control over eastern Poland and the Baltic states. He demanded territorial concessions from Finland and initiated a war of conquest that came up against unexpected resistance. On 11 May 1940 the *Wehrmacht* invaded the Netherlands and then Belgium. On 22 June, Pétain signed France's capitulation to Germany.

An emergency conference of the Fourth International was held in May 1940, at a time when the swastika was already flying over Vienna, Prague, Warsaw, Oslo, Copenhagen, The Hague and Brussels. Delegates gathered from the USA, Germany, Belgium, Canada, Mexico, Spain, Cuba, Argentina, Puerto Rico and Chile. The conference Manifesto would be the final programmatic document to which Trotsky personally contributed. In an August 1937 article, he had predicted that "war may break out within three or four years [...] To be sure, we offer this timeframe only to indicate the general tendencies at play. Political events might shorten or lengthen this timeline, but the inevitability of war stems from the economic dynamic and the dynamic of the arms race." This war foretold would be "totalitarian". The coming convulsions would "alter the face of the entire world." The most likely outcome is that "the United States will come to dominate the planet."

He warned against the illusions of those who portrayed the coming war as a crusade led by the democracies against dictatorship. The policy of non-intervention in Spain and the capitulation at Munich showed that it would be nothing of the sort. Rather, it would be an inter-imperialist conflict for a "new division of the world." Following the "imperialist peace" of Munich, "the flagrant disproportion between the specific weight of France and England in world economy and the colossal dimensions of their colonial possessions, is as much the source of global conflicts as the insatiable greed of the fascist aggressors. To put it better, the two phenomena are but two sides of the same coin." This did not imply any sort of neutrality on the question of the forms of imperialist domination – just as, from the point of view of the conditions for proletarian struggle and organization, one cannot claim there is no difference between fascist dictatorship and parliamentary democracy.

The German-Soviet Pact of August 1939 did not come as a surprise. From 1933 onwards, Trotsky had repeatedly stated that Stalin was seeking an understanding with Hitler; he had argued that the 1935 turn to the popular fronts had been nothing more than the stopgap improvisation of a rejected suitor. Kremlin policy was not based on principles but on the interests of the bureaucracy. It pragmatically adapted to the relationship of forces. The capitulation to Hitler at Munich foreshadowed the reversal in alliances that surprised so many people. In March 1939, Trotsky interpreted Stalin's speeches as "a link in the chain of a new policy in the process of formation" and as a "unilateral proposal of hand and heart" to Nazi Germany. Hitler and Stalin were "twin stars".

In a September 1939 interview with the London-based *Daily Herald*, Trotsky once again declared that world war was unavoidable. Victory for the revolution in Spain had been the last hope of avoiding it. "World War Two has begun," he said at the time, because the USA cannot remain outside the struggle for global hegemony. But Germany was too much of a latecomer on the scene of the grand imperial dividing up of the world. "The military fury that has taken hold of German imperialism will end in a terrible catastrophe. But before that, many things will have taken place in Europe." The Emergency Conference provided a summary of these positions: "The immediate cause of the present war is the rivalry between the old wealthy colonial empires, Great Britain and France, and the belated imperialist plunderers, Germany and Italy [...] This is not our war!" Against national defence in the name of anti-fascism, the Conference declaration called for the revolutionary destruction of the national state, the Socialist United States of Europe, and class fraternization between workers in uniform.

An Allied victory would mean the break-up of Germany and a new Versailles peace with the United States demanding the price of their victory. The defeat of the USSR would mean not only the overthrow of the totalitarian bureaucracy but also the collapse of the first experience of planned economy, and the transformation of the country into a colony. The least likely outcome – a peace with neither victors nor vanquished – would mean international chaos. The capitalist world would have no other perspective beyond prolonged agony.

Defence of the USSR

Debate on the question of the war was continuously intertwined with debate on the characterization and defence of the USSR. At the second congress of the French POI (Internationalist Workers Party) in November 1937, Yvan Craipeau had argued that the Soviet bureaucracy had become a class in its own right. On this basis, he determined it was necessary to abandon the position of defending the USSR as a "degenerated workers state". Trotsky responded that it did not suffice to define the bureaucracy as a class to "avoid the necessity of analyzing what place the new society occupies in the historic rise of humanity." War between Japan and Germany, on the one hand, and the Soviet Union, on the other, would put into play "the fate of the nationalized property and planned economy." The victory of the imperialist states in such a conflict would not only lead to the overthrow of the "new exploiting class" but also to the lowering of the entire Soviet economy to the level of a backward and semi-colonial capitalism. One could no more remain neutral with such stakes involved as one could when dealing with a war between a colonized country and a colonial power.

Trotsky did not exclude the "possibility of the restoration of a new possessing class arising out of the bureaucracy," but in his view this still remained only "a question of a historic possibility and not of an already accomplished fact." In such circumstances, he felt it was an abstraction to say that social-patriotism was the main danger in the USSR and on this basis demand that one choose between the "unconditional defence of the USSR" and "revolutionary defeatism". However, the analogy between defence of the USSR as a workers state and support for a colonized country against a colonial power created some ambiguity – since this meant that the "working-class" character of the state was apparently not the decisive factor.

The debate took a different turn in light of the German-Soviet Pact and the coming war. How was the agreement signed by Ribbentrop in Moscow to be understood? How to judge the USSR's policy in Poland, Finland and the Baltic states? Should the USSR continue to be defended militarily or was this new kind of patriotic *union sacrée* merely a recurrence of previous chauvinistic excesses? And if the USSR should be defended, was it because of its characterization as a workers state or in line with pragmatic criteria comparable to those which apply in a war of national-liberation between oppressors and oppressed? Or should one oppose Great Russian oppression of Poland, even if that meant advocating revolutionary defeatism in Russia as in France and Germany?

Those belonging to the current of the Socialist Workers Party (US section of the Fourth International) led by Max Shachtman and James Burnham soon came to dominate this debate. They were supported on the US-based International Executive Committee by Mario Pedrosa from Brazil (to whom honorary membership card number one was issued by the new Brazilian Workers Party – PT – in 1980) and by the Trinidadian revolutionary C.L.R James, author of the classic work *The Black Jacobins*. For Shachtman and Burnham, after its invasion of Finland the USSR could no longer be described as a degenerated workers state, and had become an imperialist state. For Trotsky, the struggle for the revolutionary overthrow of the bureaucratic dictatorship and the defence of the USSR were not incompatible, but rather complimentary.

In April 1940, the minority current led by Shachtman and Burnham left the SWP to form the Workers Party. A month later, Burnham drifted away from the new party and authored his famous essay on the managerial revolution – largely inspired by Bruno

Rizzi's book on *The Bureaucratization of the World* published in France in 1939. Pierre Naville recalled having read Burnham's *The Managerial Revolution* in 1945: "I immediately recognized the main ideas to be those of Rizzi, but lacking the originality and vitality of thought." For Rizzi, fascism, Stalinism and the New Deal all belonged to the category of "bureaucratic collectivism" and were part of a tendency towards the bureaucratization of the world. This new emerging order would be progressive. The idea of bureaucratic collectivism contains ambiguities that are symmetrical to those of the elastic notion of totalitarianism. Both notions allow for painting markedly different social relations with the same brush. Trotsky's theoretical requirements were far more stringent.

Beginning in December 1940, Shachtman – now the leader of the new Workers Party – adopted Burnham's theses. Neither a workers state nor a capitalist state, the Soviet Union was a new exploitative society led by a new bureaucratic ruling class. He saw an irreconcilable antagonism between two classes – old and new, bourgeoisie and bureaucracy. If the bureaucracy comes to play a progressive role in spite of itself, alignment with the "socialist camp" can be justified in spite of the Kremlin's crimes. If the bourgeoisie and parliamentary democracies are the ones that represent a progressive force, it is legitimate to march behind their banner in the anti-totalitarian crusade. This laid the groundwork for two opposing forms of "campism" in accordance with the binary logic of the law of the "excluded middle" (*Tertium non datur*). In Burnham's case, this led to support for McCarthyism and the US war in Vietnam.

Following the signing of the German-Soviet Pact, Trotsky reminded followers that the Fourth International – from its foundation onwards, and to the great indignation of the "friends of the USSR" – had advocated "the need to overthrow the bureaucracy through a revolutionary insurrection of the workers." Describing the bureaucracy as a caste, he stressed its "shut in character, its arbitrary rule and the haughtiness of the ruling stratum," but also that "this definition does not of course possess a strictly scientific character." Beyond the terminological squabble, it was a matter of knowing whether the bureaucracy represented "a temporary growth on a social organism." Or had it already "become transformed into a historically indispensable organ" with the ability to create a new mode of production – thereby opening a third way between capitalism and socialism in the history of humanity? While the Stalinist bureaucracy survived longer than expected, its decomposition, disastrous end and subsequent conversion to Mafia-style capitalism have confirmed the negative response to this latter question.

Two major alternative theories to Trotsky's position were developed. One characterized the Soviet regime as a "state capitalism" that inaugurated a new era following on the heels of competitive market capitalism. The other spoke of "bureaucratic collectivism", in which the bureaucracy was said to represent a new class that had created a new form of slavery for the benefit of a totalitarian exploiter. Trotsky did not hesitate to speak of a totalitarian dictatorship (*"La société, c'est moi!"* -- "I am the society!") when describing the Stalinist regime. But he insisted on the fact that this "totalitarian regime can be only a temporary transitional regime," and not a new form for the organic development of modern societies.

Trotsky explained that the slogan "defence of the USSR" did not mean defence of those characteristics it shared with capitalist countries – but rather of those which still made it different from them. For this reason, "the overthrow of the bureaucracy is indispensable for the preservation of state property," and "only in this sense do we stand for the defence of the USSR." This approach did not involve even the slightest rapprochement with the Kremlin bureaucracy. "As a matter of fact, we defend the USSR as we defend the colonies, as we solve all our problems, not by supporting some imperialist governments against others, but by the method of international class struggle in the colonies as well as in the metropolitan centres." The repeated analogy between defence of the USSR and defence of the colonized countries points to an unresolved difficulty whose roots lie in the attempt to characterize political forms in an explicitly social manner.

In the territories occupied by the USSR, Trotsky argued that it was likely that "the Moscow government will carry through the expropriation and statification of the means of production." This would be a revolutionary measure applied by military and bureaucratic means. Any independent mobilization of the masses would doubtless be quelled (and this is what indeed happened in East Berlin in 1953, Budapest in 1956, Prague in 1968 and Poland in 1976). "The primary political criterion for us is not the transformation of property relations in this or another area, however important these may be in themselves, but rather the change in the consciousness and organization of the world proletariat, the raising of their capacity for defending former conquests and accomplishing new ones. From this one, and the only decisive standpoint, the politics of Moscow, taken as a whole, wholly retain their reactionary character and remain the chief obstacle on the road to the world revolution."

So while Trotsky rejected simplified readings of a situation torn asunder by profound contradictions, he still drew a globally negative balance sheet of Stalinism. The extension of the territories under the domination of the parasitic bureaucracy might increase the Kremlin's prestige and feed illusions about the possibility of replacing revolution with bureaucratic manoeuvres from above. "This evil by far outweighs the progressive content of Stalinist reforms in Poland." This is why he was categorically opposed to the Soviet annexation of new territories such as those of western Ukraine. However, should Hitler turn his arms against Russia it would be necessary to make "military resistance against Hitler advance to the forefront as the most urgent task of the hour," because "we cannot cede to Hitler the overthrowing of Stalin; that is our own task."

On the question of whether one could describe the Kremlin's expansionist policy as "imperialist", as Burnham argued, Trotsky argued that one first had to come to some agreement around the historical meaning of the term. History had seen different sorts of imperialism (whether under slavery or feudalism, or driven by landed, commercial or industrial interests). One could speak of bureaucratic imperialism, provided that one highlight not only the similarities but also the differences. It would be more accurate to define the Kremlin's policy as that of the "Bonapartist bureaucracy of a degenerated workers state encircled by imperialism." He said that while the formula was not as high sounding as simply "imperialism", it was more correct. Of course, it was very tempting to call for insurrection on two fronts in Poland – against Hitler and against Stalin. But the concrete question was to know what to do if Hitler invaded the USSR before the revolution had settled Stalin's fate. If he did, one would have to fight Hitler's troops as one fought in the Republican army in Spain against the Francoist uprising – all the while safeguarding the programmatic and organizational independence of the Fourth International.

Defencism, defeatism, neutralism and resistance

The primary concern of the *Emergency Manifesto* was to avoid a repeat of the August 1914 *union sacrée* based on an alleged conflict between democracy and fascism. For the defeated and occupied countries, however, Trotsky foresaw a worsening of social conditions for the masses and the possibility of movements of resistance against national oppression: "France is being transformed into an oppressed nation," he wrote in June 1940 in one of his last articles. But he refused to adapt the "old arguments of social patriotism" to the new map of Europe: "Should the working class tie up its fate in the present war with the fate of imperialist democracy, it would only assure itself a new series of defeats." In this way, he kept a safeguard in place while simultaneously stressing that national oppression and territorial occupation did indeed represent new factors in the war. When a country is occupied, it is not enough to declare that "the enemy is at home" and advocate revolutionary defeatism against the *union sacrée*. This is the challenge that Trotskyists would face – equipped with a heritage that was invaluable but which came without a clear set of instructions.

The problem was not resolved by the International's repeated proclamations of independence in relation to the official resistance in France and Yugoslavia. Though necessary to guard against the danger of a drift towards nationalism, this independence was insufficient for charting a practical political orientation. The German invasion of the USSR and China's resistance against Japan further accentuated the complexity of the war and the stakes involved. The Fourth International resolution on the March 1941 American intervention in China recognized China's need to accept US assistance while not ignoring the dangers this involved, since "the fact that the war between Japanese and American imperialism (in which Chiang Kai-shek will be a subordinate ally of the latter) will possess a purely imperialist character, does not wipe out the problems of China's struggle to expel the Japanese invaders." This cautious position clearly reflected the hesitations and divisions of the Chinese Trotskyists themselves – between either adopting a purely class policy leading to abstention on the national question, or forming a perilous alliance with the Maoist resistance. From the invasion of Russia onwards, FI documents call for boycotts and sabotage of the countries fighting the USSR, but not of countries allied to it.

Following the French debacle of 1940, Trotskyist organizations were compelled to adjust perspectives elaborated at the time of World War One. In this respect, the evolution of Marcel Hic – leader of the French section until his capture and deportation in October 1943 – is telling. In 1941, he saw mass support for De Gaulle as "something essentially healthy." At the underground congress of the Internationalist Workers Party (POI) in 1943, he looked back at the "unfortunate nationalist illusions" of the Trotskyist press at the beginning of the war. But it was never a question of neutrality, a charge frequently levelled against Trotskyists. In September 1940, the bulletin of the French Committees for the Fourth International declared, "France is on the way to becoming an oppressed country. We want a free France, a French France, in a socialist Europe." It called for the creation of "committees of national vigilance", "organs of national struggle", and for "organized passive resistance" around democratic slogans such as: "Down with the pillage of French wealth!", "Release the prisoners!", "Withdrawal from French territory!", and "For a united, free, independent France!". At the same time, far from embracing anti-German feeling, they pursued fraternization with German workers in uniform – "misled brothers" – while simultaneously declaring themselves to be "merciless adversaries of Nazis in uniform."

The *Theses on the National Question*, drafted by Marcel Hic in July 1942 for the European Secretariat, proclaimed that the struggle for national demands in France is "inseparable from full support for the struggle of colonial peoples against imperialism." It restated support for national demands, including the rights of linguistic communities (whether Breton, Basque, Flemish, Walloon, Ukrainian or Albanian) to run their own affairs, administer justice and be taught in their own languages. These theses refute the old yarn about the indifference of Trotskyists (and Marxists more generally) to the national question. The theses advocate "participation in all mass national uprisings" around one's own slogans. In December 1943, a European Secretariat resolution argued that the partisan movement created a political opening for the masses and could provide military assistance to the Soviet Union. It called on supporters to "play the role of armed detachments of the proletarian revolution and not of reinforcements for the imperialist army; to be autonomously self-organized along democratic lines and to the exclusion of all bourgeois and reactionary forces; to set up secret factions within the military organizations controlled by the *union sacrée*; to oppose any policy of assassinating German soldiers and any act of sabotage that would create a chasm between the native working class and German soldiers; to carry out propaganda work aimed at fraternization with the occupying troops; and to welcome German deserters into their ranks."

Disagreements with the official resistance were not about the need to fight the occupier, but rather the methods employed. The Trotskyists in the POI opposed minority military actions and stressed the need for mass resistance and self-organization. Their approach might seem unrealistic given the forces involved and the fact that attempts to join the resistance movement came up against Stalinist repression – as exemplified by the 1943 assassination of

Pietro Tresso and his comrades after their escape from the Le Puy jail in the south of France (an episode described by Pierre Broué, Alain Dugrand and Raymond Vacheron in the book *Meurtres au maquis*).

In 1943, Stalin formally announced the dissolution of the Third International. Around the same time, the European Secretariat of the Fourth International set about organizing a conference, which was held in February 1944. The Conference resolution asserted that "the proletariat cannot disregard the struggle of the masses against the oppression of German imperialism," but also symmetrically criticized the "social-patriotic deviation" of the POI (the French section recognized at the beginning of the war) and the "left-sectarian deviation" of the smaller Internationalist Communist Committee (CCI). The POI was criticized for not distinguishing between "the imperialist nationalism of the defeated bourgeoisie" and the nationalism of masses giving reactionary expression to their resistance against exploitation and German imperialist occupation. Instead, the POI had seen as progressive the struggle of its own bourgeoisie "without distancing itself from Gaullism." Conversely, the CCI had refused to distinguish between "the nationalism of the bourgeoisie and the mass resistance movement." With respect to the partisan movement of resistance, the statement added: "When it is a matter of tactical units set up by nationalist and Stalinist patriotic organizations, our attitude towards such units is based on their objectives and the results of their action." These formulations provide a good illustration of the contradictions small groups of activists face in the midst of a huge free-for-all involving colossal forces. Their efforts were all the more honourable in that these activists were exposed to the twofold peril of the repression of the occupier and – within the resistance movement itself – the criminal hostility of the Stalinists.

The clandestine POI's publication *La Vérité* (The Truth) reappeared in August 1940, printed on a mimeograph machine. The preoccupation with fighting chauvinism within the working-class movement was given concrete expression in 1943 with the publication of *Arbeiter und Soldat* (Worker and Soldier), a special bulletin meant for German occupation troops. From early 1944 onwards, *La Vérité* condemned plans to "carve up Germany." On 17 February 1944, it put out a call for "help for the lads in the *maquis* (resistance movement)" and to "shoot members of the militia like rabid dogs." The 29 April 1944 issue ran the headline: "From protest movement to armed struggle". The 1 May 1944 special issue called for a May Day general strike, and called on workers to seize the occasion of the Allied landing to occupy the factories and mines to establish workers control over production and transport, and to struggle for the socialist United States of Europe.

While the POI's criticism of the leadership of the resistance focussed on their methods and not on the principle of resistance itself, the position of the CCI was more abstentionist, as was that of the group created around the *Lutte de classe* (Class Struggle) journal, forerunner of today's Lutte Ouvrière (LO - Worker's Struggle) group. This group was initially set up by a handful of people around David Korner (also known as Barta), a Romanian Jew who, having tried in vain to enter Republican Spain, got active in the POI where he supported the minority in favour of joining Marceau Pivert's PSOP. He parted ways with the International and its French section before the war, accusing them of tailing Communist Parties and left Social Democrats at the expense of their own political and organizational independence. His group saw a resistance movement rife with "class-collaborationist trickery" ; their bulletin drummed out slogans against imperialist war that were directly inspired by revolutionary defeatism inherited from the time of the First World War. The first issue of *Lutte de Classe* launched a campaign against the Nazi forced labour program in France (STO). The campaign's main leader, Mathieu Bucholtz, was murdered by Stalinists in September 1944. Issue number 25 in February 1944 ran its headline on the execution of the Manouchian resistance group: "Defend the terrorists". In his editorial, Barta wrote, "Look at them closely, these faces of the oppressed and exploited, these faces of workers from many different countries [...] Their courage must serve as an example."

The war broke the generational and organizational continuity of Trotskyist organizations. By war's end, they had lost most of the movement's pioneers and founding members – as a result of repression, exhaustion or demoralization. There were victims not only of fascist and colonial repression, but also of Stalinist repression – including Trotsky himself, who finally fell to assassins in Mexico City in August 1940.

4. *The scattering of the tribes*

Like the prophecies of the ancient prophets (taking the form of "if-then" statements), Trotsky's forecasts were conditional rather than divinatory. They did not declare with certainty what would occur, but put forward strategic hypotheses for action. In a February 1940 interview, Trotsky asserted that "the war will spread until it exhausts all of civilization's resources, or instead until its back is broken by the revolution." Either, or. If, then.

Between these different alternatives, he allowed for a wide range of possible outcomes. In August 1937, he proclaimed: "Everything suggests that if humanity as a whole is not plunged into barbarism, the social bases of the Soviet regime (the property forms of the planned economy) will survive the ordeal of the war and will even emerge strengthened." However, in October 1938 following Munich, he envisioned another outcome: "Naturally, if a new war ends only in a military victory of this or that imperialist camp; if a war calls forth neither a revolutionary uprising nor a victory of the proletariat; if a new imperialist peace more terrible than the Versailles treaty places new chains for decades upon the people; if unfortunate humanity bears all this in silence and submission [...] In this eventuality, the further frightful decomposition of capitalism will cast all humanity back for many decades. Of course in the realization of *this* perspective of passivity, capitulation, defeat, and decline, the oppressed classes and entire peoples must then climb on all fours in sweat and in blood over the historic road already once traversed."

One year later, in *The USSR in War*, he considered other hypotheses: "The inability of the proletariat to take into its hands the leadership of society could actually lead under these conditions to the growth of a new exploiting class from the Bonapartist fascist bureaucracy. This would be, according to all indications, a regime of decline, signalling the eclipse of civilization. An analogous result might occur in the event that the proletariat of advanced capitalist countries, having conquered power, should prove incapable of holding it and surrender it, as in the USSR, to a privileged bureaucracy. Then we would be compelled to acknowledge that the reason for the bureaucratic relapse is rooted not in the backwardness of the country and not in the imperialist environment but in the congenital incapacity of the proletariat to become a ruling class. Then it would be necessary in retrospect to establish that in its fundamental traits the present USSR was the precursor of a new exploiting regime on an international scale." Bureaucratic collectivism was therefore a feasible prospect; were it to come about, Trotsky argued, it would necessarily lead to a radical break with the Marxist paradigm. This is far removed from a teleological and unidirectional view of history: "[...] Either the Stalin regime is an abhorrent relapse in the process of transforming bourgeois society into a socialist society, or the Stalin regime is the first stage of a new exploiting society." Faced with such an outcome, he said, our descendants would have to define their politics in radically new conditions.

Trotsky's dialectical prophecies have been debated as fiercely in the Trotskyist microcosm as those of Nostradamus have been among Estericists. Following the war, his heirs were confronted with a series of major questions.

1. *The first concerned the analysis of the period.* Though not widely influential, the theses put forward by two leaders of the German section were symptomatic of the looming demoralization. They predicted a long war that would destroy civilization. In such conditions, developed European nations would come to endure national oppression that would leave them worse off than India. The prospect of revolution was therefore put off to some distant future date, with the immediate task being that of defending democratic gains. This kind of historical pessimism could only lead to the politics of lesser evilism, subordinated to either the Western democracies or the Kremlin bureaucracy.

Instead of correcting pre-war analyses in light of unforeseeable factors such as the nuclear balance of terror, the main approach among leaders of the International in Europe and the USA was to see the post-war period as a break or interlude from a war that would continue in different ways. They consequently saw no reason to alter their previous strategic outlook. However, the American leader Felix Morrow had already drawn attention to the strategic error of placing exclusive emphasis on "objectively" revolutionary conditions. He argued that the absence of a mass revolutionary party was not merely the missing piece of a puzzle; rather, it qualitatively transformed "conditions which would otherwise be revolutionary." This remark challenges a formulation in the *Transitional Program* according to which the crisis of humanity is reduced to the crisis of its revolutionary leadership. The formulation might have been relatively accurate in the 1930s, when there was a powerful working-class movement and the effects of the dynamic created by the October revolution were still being felt. But the cumulative dynamic of defeats ultimately changed the objective conditions themselves.

In 1947, the young Belgian economist Ernest Mandel argued that the boom would be short-lived and would be followed by a new revolutionary upsurge. While he would later come to analyze the inner workings of the world economy's long expansive wave, others – such as the Lambertist current – would seek to remain loyal to the conjunctural formulation in the *Transitional Program* that "the productive forces stagnate." They would do so in defiance of the facts, in the face of a full-blown technological revolution and a huge increase in the productivity of labour.

As early as 1947, others were already having doubts. In his memoirs, the founder of the International Socialism current, Tony Cliff, a Palestinian Jew who arrived in London in 1946, describes how he was struck by the country's relative prosperity. In the event – together with the Argentinean delegate Nahuel Moreno – the British delegates to the Second World Congress in 1948 tabled amendments that took note of the way the Marshall Plan had helped restore production and stabilized the relationship of forces in Europe. But the majority of the International leadership feared that forecasts of a new phase of expansion would lead to rightist capitulation. Lacking a rounded explanation for the dynamism that was in sharp contrast to the slump of the 1930s, it was indeed tempting to jettison Marxist critique in favour of Keynesian prescriptions.

2. *The explosive "Russian question"*. Establishing a parallel with the Napoleonic Wars, Trotsky had forecast that the occupation of Poland, Finland and the Baltic states by the Red Army would probably lead to their "structural assimilation" into the social relations of the Soviet Union. The transfer of property to state ownership would be relatively progressive, but in a contradictory way in as much as it would result from authoritarian decisions opposed to the autonomous mobilization of the proletariat. Were the bureaucracy to remain in power following the war, it would be a "regime of decline, signalling the eclipse of civilization" and not the advent of a new progressive mode of production.

By the end of the 1940s, it was clear that the Stalinist regime had survived. A new explanation was needed. The revived Fourth International stuck to the letter of the pre-war documents, describing the Soviet Union as a degenerated workers state. As for the states of Eastern Europe, in 1948 they had been seen as capitalist states under police dictatorship. The theses on the Soviet Union and

Stalinism considered that "what remains of the gains of October is increasingly losing its value." Each day, the parasitic bureaucracy undermined the social relations inherited from the revolution. The deadweight on the shoulders of the workers led to a relative decrease in the productivity of labour. It was a matter of understanding these real contradictions instead of denying them in favour of simplifications. In the view of the Second Congress, the USSR was therefore a society in transition from capitalism to socialism. The weakness of this formulation is that it corresponds to a linear vision of history and presents a false dilemma (*tertium non datur*) – instead of promoting an understanding of a very specific social reality. The definition of the Soviet Union as "post-capitalist" is likewise flawed. From the point of view of the totality of world social relations, the bureaucratic regime does not come "after" capitalism; on the contrary, it is its contemporary – very much a part of its time and space and dependent upon its imperialist logic.

Aware of these theoretical difficulties, the authors of the Congress documents used caution with the terms they employed and recommended the removal of terms steeped in illusion – such as those describing the USSR as the "final bastion of revolution" and characterizing its economy as a "socialist economy". They symmetrically rejected the superficial analogies contained in such vague notions as "red fascism" and "Soviet imperialism".

3. The third major question thrown up by the post-war situation concerned the Fourth International's failure to grow in line with expectations. Trotsky had predicted that it would be the central revolutionary force in the world by the time of the centenary of the Communist Manifesto in 1948. The European Conference of February 1944 had nevertheless observed shortcomings that stemmed from the movement's political immaturity: "The frequent crises, intellectualism and factionalism that have often accompanied the development of this movement are in part the consequence of a defective social make-up that long prevented it from taking full advantage of the real objective possibilities. Always looking at the purely political side of its work criticizing Stalinism and the other opportunist tendencies of the workers movement, our movement has often lost sight of the problems associated with our own organization, its social make-up, its ongoing practical work, the recruitment and education of members, and methods of functioning and organization." Having internalized their marginality, the FI's sections often existed as caretaker organizations at the expense of patient long-term work. As if to compensate for this recurring flaw, the fetishism of organizational methodology often stepped in as a

replacement for a political orientation in organizations such as the American Socialist Workers Party and Lutte Ouvrière (Workers Struggle) in France.

The ritual formulation of the Transitional Program – according to which the crisis of humanity is reduced to the crisis of its revolutionary leadership – is relatively correct in a given context. Raised to the level of a timeless truth, however, it becomes a source of political paranoia. If the supposedly excellent objective conditions do not give rise to major successes, then the explanation must be sought out in the vanguard's capitulations and betrayals. In such cases, the politics of suspicion, systematic groundless accusation and the constant fear of betrayal produce disastrous effects.

There was a quickening of events following the war. In 1944, the Germans capitulated and the Yalta Accords were signed. In 1945, atomic bombs were dropped on Japan. The year 1947 saw civil war in Greece, the expulsion of the Communist Parties from government in France and Italy, splits in the trade unions, the creation of the Kominform and the adoption of the Marshall Plan. In 1948, there was the "Prague coup", and the public break between Stalin and Tito. In 1949, there was the victory of the Chinese Revolution, the proclamation of the East German republic, the formation of NATO and the first steps toward the 1951 creation of the European common market for coal and steel. Partially confirming pre-war forecasts, the world was shaken by upheavals in France, in Italy until 1948, in Greece, and especially in China and Yugoslavia. The colonial revolution was on the move in Vietnam, Indonesia and India. But the industrialized countries remained prisoners of the great "carve up" that took place at Yalta – a term that takes on a literal and mathematical meaning when one looks at the haggling that took place with Stalin, as related by Churchill in his memoirs. Compelled to put down their arms in compliance with the Treaty of Varkiza, the Greek Communists were Yalta's first casualties.

However, the partial confirmations of the pre-war strategic outlook could not mask the fact that it had been invalidated in overall terms. Crushed and left leaderless by Hitler, battered by Allied bombing raids, neutralized by the partitioning of Germany, the German proletariat had not recovered. The Soviet regime had survived by putting the proletariat and whole peoples through a terrible bloodletting. The imperialist economies experienced a difficult recovery, and were not plunged into a crisis without end. Not only did they not disappear, in fact the old Social Democratic and Stalinist parties took centre stage once again. The political explanation for this situation resided in the compromise between the imperialist victors and the Stalinist bureaucracy, in the division of Europe into zones of influence, in the concessions wrenched from frightened bourgeois classes in search of a new social compromise, and in the loosening of the colonial vice in some countries. All this helped contain the first revolutionary wave. Still, the Trotskyists were now faced with a situation that they had not anticipated.

The international conference held in Paris in April 1946 restored the International's ties with its contacts abroad. It upheld the forecast of an enduring economic slump that would come on the heels of a short-lived recovery. The perspective of imminent revolution was also upheld, though postponed somewhat. The points of self-criticism relate to the "tempo and not the fundamental character of the period [...] Only the superficial and cowardly petty-bourgeois mind can see a refutation of our revolutionary perspective in these facts: that war did not, either during its course or immediately thereafter, bring about the revolution in Europe; that the German revolution has not taken place; that the traditional organizations, and foremost among them, the Stalinist parties, have experienced a new and powerful rise. While recognizing that all of these facts represent so many defeats for the revolutionary proletariat, the Fourth International cannot for one moment forget that the mortal crisis of capitalism, the destruction of its equilibrium, the sharpening of all of its fundamental contradictions, constitute far more important facts, and upon them rest our revolutionary perspective and our vastly increased opportunities for building the revolutionary party."

The unexpected turn of the world situation in 1947-1948 demanded a more radical redefinition of the International's project. This unresolved matter lay at the heart of the centrifugal dynamics that beset the international Trotskyist movement at the time. It had already become a bone of contention by the time of the 1948 World Congress, which met at the very beginning of the Cold War – soon after the "Prague coup" and shortly before the Soviet-Yugoslav split and the victory of the Chinese Revolution. While there were disagreements about the potential for recovery of the capitalist economies, still no one ventured to predict that they were on the onset of a long 30-year period of post-war economic boom. Turning back to the long forgotten theory of cycles and long waves, Ernest Mandel devoted the better part of his published work (*Marxist Economic Theory* in 1962 [1968 in English translation] and *Late Capitalism* in 1975) to uncovering the secret of this capitalist dynamism. As for the question of imminent war, this did not come off as the hair-brained imaginings of doomsayers but rather as an entirely conceivable development – coming on the eve of the Chinese Revolution and the Korean War, and just as the USSR was on the verge of acquiring nuclear arms.

However, the debates of the Congress centred primarily on the events in Eastern Europe and on the nature of the states under Soviet authority. The Cold War was pushing the USSR to "structurally assimilate" the occupied countries – that is, to forcibly align their social relations with those of the Soviet Union. The Congress majority argued that these countries were capitalist countries under occupation by a police dictatorship. One year later, in 1949, these countries were described as being "on the path of incomplete structural assimilation". The awkwardness of the formulation spoke to a clear difficulty. Between 1948 and 1950, the situation quickly unravelled. In June 1948, the Stalin-Tito split became public. Structural assimilation took shape in response to plans for a Balkan federation that could have asserted a degree of independence from the Kremlin. In April 1950, Ernest Mandel came over to the characterization of Yugoslavia as a workers state, but continued to describe the other countries under Soviet control as degenerated bourgeois states. The Chinese Communist Party continued to be defined as a "Stalinist-led peasant movement".

In the USSR, the thirty years that had gone by since the revolution were described as "proving the extraordinary solidity of the new social relations". This highly debatable appreciation accurately reflects the bewilderment of delegates at the Second Congress in the face of the unexpected resilience of the Stalinist regime – under which "reaction and regression in all fields [...] have been shown to be infinitely vaster and more dangerous than anyone could have thought." A united, socialist Europe was seen as being the only progressive alternative to the Marshall Plan and the partitioning of the continent. Consequently, the Congress called for the unconditional unification of Germany and for the withdrawal of Soviet troops from the "buffer states" under Soviet occupation. It considered that Washington was preparing for war against the USSR, not to introduce political democracy there but to restore capitalism. The title of the Congress Manifesto accurately summarizes the gathering's general orientation: "Against Wall Street and the Kremlin!"

Disillusionment soon led to the first significant defections from the Trotskyist movement. In 1947, David Rousset – who had been expelled from the French section in 1945 for his crypto-Stalinist views – founded the short-lived Rassemblement démocratique révolutionnaire (RDR) with Jean-Paul Sartre. The RDR began to disintegrate soon after organizing a conference against dictatorship in war in April 1948 – at which the American delegate sang the praises of the atomic bomb's dissuasive effects in the face of Soviet expansionism. The pro-RDR split from the FI led by Paul Parisot, Albert Demazières and Louis Dalmas nonetheless took more than a third of the members of the French section.

The Second Congress also learned of the letter sent by Trotsky's widow, Natalia Sedova, and the poet Benjamin Péret. It put its finger on the questions taunting Trotskyists everywhere: "The policies of Russia and Stalinism beat down much more heavily upon human hope than the financial capitalism of Wall Street." Defence of the USSR, they argued, was damaging the world revolution much more than it was contributing to it. This "destructive loyalty" must be abandoned. This is "the most important point of contention in our movement." The two authors, who would leave the International after the Congress, concluded their letter by declaring: "Down with Trotskyist conservatism! Down with Trotskyist fetishism!"

Max Shachtman was a Congress delegate and also subsequently left the International for good. By 1947, he was arguing that Stalinism was worse than capitalism and considered Social Democracy to be a lesser evil. This shift in thinking led him to embrace the Atlantic alliance at the end of the 1940s and to drift towards "liberal anti-totalitarianism" or "liberal (and no longer solely anti-Stalinist) anti-communism". He ended up joining the Democratic Party and supporting the intervention in Vietnam. A minority of his current opposed this trajectory and in 1964 founded the Independent Socialist Clubs, going on to join the British *International Socialism* current in 1969 and the Solidarity network in 1985. As for Burnham, he continued his drift by backing the idea of a preventive nuclear war against the USSR during the Cold War and supporting the American intervention in Vietnam. As Trotsky had foreseen, Burnham's analysis of the proletariat's powerlessness had led him to dismiss Marxism in general as utopian.

Having left Cannon's SWP in 1940 to join Shachtman's Workers Party, the tendency led by Johnson and Forrest (respectively the pseudonyms of C.L.R James and Raya Dunayevskaya) took the opposite tack in 1949. Originally from Trinidad, James had moved to the USA in 1938. In his view, the social base of Stalinism was the petty bourgeoisie in the era of state capitalism. It was not a phenomenon confined to the Soviet Union, but rather a universal tendency that corresponded to the new organization of production and the underlying convergence between the social systems of the East and West. In their draft resolution for the Second Congress,

Johnson and Forrest argued that, in spite of the heroism of its members, the Fourth International had remained a sect torn between Stalinophobia and Stalinophilia. By nurturing Keynesian illusions in the potential for state regulation of the market, the nationalizations of the post-war period were leading the working class astray. To counter these broad trends, they advocated spontaneous forms of self-organization.

Cornelius Castoriadis had broken with the Greek CP in 1942. He put forward his own minority position at the Second Congress, under the pseudonym Chaulieu. He argued that the notion of the degenerated workers state confused property relations with relations of production. Social relations in the USSR remained relations of exploitation in which capital was appropriated by the ruling bureaucracy. The notion of the degenerated workers state, which earlier may have been justified, had become inoperative at least since 1928 and the first five-year plan. Castoriadis concluded from this that the USSR was merging capital with the state and leading towards world domination by a single state; and that the CPs were becoming agents of a third way, beyond the divide between capitalism and socialism. Along with C.L.R James, to whom he felt close, Castoriadis did not consider Stalinism to be an historical accident produced by the pressure of the world market and a capitalist environment on a workers state. Rather, he saw it as a new phase of capitalist development. He therefore preferred the term "bureaucratic capitalism" over that of "state capitalism" – all the better to emphasize that one was dealing with a new and unexpected stage of historical development. He sought out an alternative in councilist and self-management experiences, stressing the voluntarist invention of new forms of organization and new institutions as opposed to the dialectic of needs and the dynamic of social contradictions. He also argued for revolutionary defeatism in case of war, as opposed to the traditional position of defending the USSR.

Castoriadis also left the International and in early 1949 formed the *Socialisme ou barbarie* journal and group with Claude Lefort, Jean François Lyotard and Daniel Mothé. The question of Stalinism was the main reason for the break. Why was the Fourth International unable to break radically with Stalinism, contenting itself with a role of subordinate opposition instead of asserting a truly autonomous project? *Socialisme ou barbarie* rejected the policy of the so-called workers united front that they argued gave cover to this adaptation to Stalinism, and sought to build unitary rank-and-file workplace committees instead of getting active in the trade unions. The group also condemned support for the Yugoslav revolution and set out to provide a new theorization of the nature of the bureaucratized states. In spite of its radical character, the group remained on the margins. It practically disappeared after it disbanded in 1966. In the 1980s, Castoriadis presented an amplified version of his original ideas in his book *Devant la guerre*, in which the all-powerful Soviet "statocracy" is described as the main threat to the future of humanity. Bureaucratic totalitarianism is worse than military dictatorships, he argued, since the latter come and go while the former is eternal.

Tony Cliff also left the International after the 1948 Congress. He advanced an alternative overall analysis of the new situation around three ideas: state capitalism in the East, the role of the permanent arms economy in the world and deflected permanent revolution in the colonial countries.

The Soviet state was not a workers state but state capitalist.

The newfound economic dynamism did not signify the triumph of Keynesian measures; it resulted from growth sustained by the permanent arms economy.

In this international context, permanent revolution in colonial countries was channelled towards the formation of statified economies run by new bureaucratic elites.

Cliff systematized his position in the 1955 book *State Capitalism in Russia*. In his eyes, October 1917 remained an authentic revolution; but a workers state should be characterized by the organization of the proletariat as a ruling class and not by state property of the means of production – by the degree of self-organization and self-activity of the class, and not according to the legal status of property relations. He considered that with the theory of structural assimilation the "Bismarckian" path for the structural transformation of social relations from above tended to become the rule. Could one still speak of a workers state when the workers remained separated from the means of production? Dogmatic adherence to outdated formulations, he argued, stemmed from a fetishization of property relations! Such an approach, he continued, led one to see the anti-bureaucratic revolution not as a genuinely new revolution but rather as a self-reform of the bureaucratic system. Property relations could not be separated from the relations of production that encompass them. From this came the slogan "Neither Moscow nor Washington but International Socialism!" This theory of state capitalism, which remains on the terrain of Marxist categories, places greater emphasis on the similarities between capitalism and the regime produced by the bureaucratic counter-revolution than on their structural differences. But this ran up against a contradiction: if they were the international agents of state capitalism, why were the Stalinist parties able to have so much influence over the working class? Was this a sign that a majority segment of the proletariat preferred the security of this new alienation over the uncertainties of self-emancipation?

These controversies were the expression of a major theoretical difficulty. Beginning in the 1930s, workers in the Soviet Union were definitely not masters of the means of production. But nor was their labour power a commodity in the same way as in the capitalist countries; and the surplus labour extracted from them was not accumulated in the form of capital but consumed unproductively in the form of privileges, waste and arms expenditure. For Cliff, the essential characteristics of the capitalist mode of production are the separation of workers from the means of production and the fact that labour power takes the commodity form. According to him, these two conditions were met in the USSR with the 1929-1932 five-year plan. During this period, he argued, the USSR became state capitalist. The purges and trials only served to consolidate this transformation. The bureaucracy had transformed itself into a full blown ruling class.

Similarly, the theory of permanent revolution was put to the test of the Chinese revolution and, later, the Cuban revolution. How was one to define regimes born of a seizure of power by parties opposed to the autonomy of the social movements – as had been the case in China, with the Maoist leadership's call for quiet in the cities during the 1949 military offensive; and as had been partially the case in Cuba, with the tensions between the "*selva*" (the jungle) and the "*llano*" (the plain) described by Carlos Franqui in his *Diary of the Cuban Revolution*.

The main leaders of the international majority, Michel Pablo and Ernest Mandel, took the opposite tack and attempted to take stock of new developments while sticking closely to an orthodox outlook. They used the development of the productive forces in the USSR as an argument, in as much as this was meant to prove the superiority of even an imperfect socialization of the means of production. This argument eventually became a double-edged sword, when the growth rates of the period of extensive accumulation gave way to the stagnation and regression of the Brezhnev era. Taking the argument further, in 1956 Isaac Deutscher forecast that in less than ten years the USSR would surpass the standard of living in the USA. At the end of the 1950s, in the midst of Sputnik-inspired euphoria, the idea of catching up to and surpassing the USA in the run-up to the new century was a central part of Kruschevian rhetoric. For Cliff, however, the bureaucracy had become an almost total obstacle. The development of labour productivity was hampered not only by bureaucratic waste but also by passive resistance to alienated labour. In his final writings, he argued that the post-mortem confirmation of this thesis in the USSR came with the slowdown in growth in the 1970s, with the fact that workers had in no way defended what was supposed to have been their state, and with the fact that the bureaucracy had found a place in the world market – given that a majority of its members became active agents of capitalist restoration.

These controversies raise a number of questions about the structure of the bureaucratic counter-revolution and about directly social characterizations of political phenomena. On the one hand, looking for an event that is symmetrical to the revolutionary event – as if historical time were reversible – creates an obstacle to understanding an original process with new and unexpected developments. On the other hand, whether dealing with states or parties, applying the "workers" label attributes a social substance to them – and evades the specificity of political phenomena which themselves transform social relations. The directly social characterization of political forms then becomes a dogmatic straitjacket paralyzing all thought. Finally, it is important to point out that, however different their characterizations of the Soviet Union, every single one of the protagonists examined here considered the Russian revolution to be an authentic revolution and not a coup d'état – Pablo as much as Castoriadis, Mandel as much as Cliff, and Cannon as much as C.L.R. James. What's more, they all saw the qualitative counter-revolutionary turning point as having occurred at the time of the first five-year plan and the Great Terror of the 1930s.

5. *Waiting for Godot*[4]

At the beginning of the 1950s, the International leadership attempted to fashion a new overall political project – on the initiative of Michel Raptis, also known as Pablo. The Korean War had begun in April 1950. The 1950s were characterized by the climate of the Cold War, McCarthyism in the USA, the trial and execution of the Rosenbergs, the beginning of the experiment with self-management in Yugoslavia, and breakthroughs for the anti-colonial revolution in Egypt and Bolivia in 1952. There was the workers uprising in East Berlin in 1953; French imperialism was defeated at Dien Bien Phu in May 1954 and the Algerian war of liberation began on 1 November that same year. The following year the conference of non-aligned Asian-African states was held in Bandung, Indonesia – on the initiative of India, Egypt and Yugoslavia. In 1956, Nasser nationalized the Suez Canal; Khrushchev denounced Stalin's crimes in his report to the 20th Party Congress; Mao launched the Hundred Flowers Campaign in China; Warsaw and Budapest rose up against the bureaucratic yoke; and the Hungarian revolution was crushed by Soviet tanks. In Cuba, a dozen bearded survivors from the landing of the Granma begin the armed struggle against the Batista dictatorship.

By the beginning of the 1950s, it was clear that capitalism was not going to collapse under the weight of its contradictions, and that the Soviet bureaucracy was consolidating its hold over its satellite states. At the same time, though, the spread of the revolution to Yugoslavia and China and the rise of the anti-colonial revolution were sharpening the contradictions of the emerging world order.

The position that took shape in the International was directly linked to the expectation of an imminent new world war. This "coming war" would take the form of a worldwide civil war or of a "war-revolution". In the context of the Cold War, such a development was by no means implausible. In March 1951, Pablo published an article entitled "Where Are We Going?" in which he

---

4 In the Irish writer Samuel Beckett's most well-known work, the play *Waiting for Godot*, two characters wait for someone named Godot, who never arrives.

analyzed "objective social reality" as "made up essentially of the capitalist regime and the Stalinist world." These factors made up "the sum total of objective reality," because, whether one liked it or not, "the overwhelming majority of forces opposed to capitalism are currently led or influenced by the Soviet bureaucracy." This approach was premised on the existence of a conflict between a social system (capitalism) and a vague notion (the "Stalinist world"). This theoretical ambiguity was reinforced by the assertion that "the transition [from capitalism to socialism] will probably occupy an historical period lasting a few centuries." Stalinism therefore appeared to be part of an enduring epoch that involved a longer transition than expected from capitalism to socialism. Similar reasoning had led David Rousset, Gilles Martinet and the economist Charles Bettelheim to consider Stalinism as a strategic ally and to come to terms with it as a Hegelian ruse of historical reason.

On its own, there is nothing heretical about the "centuries of transition" formulation. While taking power is a political event, the transformation of social relations is a historical process whose duration no one can predetermine. However, when associated with a world view shaped entirely by the confrontation between imperialism and the "Stalinist world", such an analysis can become the justification for a *realpolitik* aligned with one or the other contending camp. This is why Pablo's opponents accused him of "campism" and of appeasing the Soviet bureaucracy.

A thorny question further complicated the debate: how was one to understand the Yugoslavian and Chinese revolutions and characterize their leaderships? In both cases, Trotskyists were victims of bureaucratic repression. In China, the leaders of the Trotskyist movement had been jailed as soon as the Communist Party took power in 1949. In Yugoslavia, the Belgrade Trotskyists had been liquidated in 1941. Confusing the mass movement and its leadership, an understandable Stalinophobia could have led one to draw sectarian conclusions. It was particularly laudable, therefore, not to see major historical events through the prism of the narrow interests of a group or party. As a result, unlike the structural assimilation of the satellite states, the Yugoslav and Chinese revolutions were greeted by the International majority as genuine revolutions that would inevitably come into conflict with the Kremlin's bureaucratic conservatism. To explain this, Pablo used a short sentence from the *Transitional Program* that foresaw how in "exceptional circumstances" some Stalinist parties might go further than they wished along the road to a break with the bourgeoisie. Between admitting that Stalinist parties could lead revolutions (was the building of new revolutionary parties then still necessary?) and denying that revolutions had occurred (by invoking the historical development of bureaucratic collectivism or contemplating the rapid worldwide development of petty-bourgeois revolutions), there was very little middle ground to tread.

Conscious of the dangers of this double bind, Ernest Mandel submitted his "Ten Theses" for debate in January 1951. In this document, Mandel warns against generalizations made on the basis of specific cases, which would make the building of the Fourth International meaningless. He distinguishes Soviet expansionism in the satellite states from the revolutionary conquest of power by the Chinese and Yugoslavian CPs. But the clearest response to Pablo's thesis came from the secretary of the French section, Marcel Bleibtreu, who rejected any theory of blocs and camps in which classes, states and nations would be brought together in one big jumble. He rejected predictions that the Thermidorian bureaucracy would survive indefinitely into the future – a view he saw as grist to the mill of the theory of bureaucratic collectivism. He saw the peasant and worker masses as the social base of Chinese Stalinism. He continued to defend the Soviet Union, but subordinated it to the development of the world revolution. Bleibtreu also raised a decisive question of method. The subordination of the Communist Parties to the Soviet bureaucracy was not the result of some kind of Stalinist essence turned into a metaphysical abstraction, but rather of a specific historical process that one needed to study in each concrete case. As such, the Stalinization of the French CP – completed in the early 1930s – was different from that of the underground Italian CP in exile, or that of the Spanish CP which faced competition from the anarchists and the POUM. A Communist Party that led a mass struggle for the conquest of power against Kremlin instructions could not strictly be characterized as Stalinist; doing otherwise would have meant giving more weight to ideological criteria, at the expense of social and historical analysis. This had been the case of the Communist Party of Yugoslavia, whose conflictual relations with the Kremlin from 1941 onwards and resistance to the division of the Balkans decided at Yalta only became known later. This had also been the case of the Chinese Communist Party – which, having learned the lessons of the tragedy of 1927, refused to subordinate itself to the Kuomintang in the anti-Japanese resistance and, unlike the Communist Party of Greece, refused to hand over its arms at the Chungking talks of August-October 1945, at a time when the Kremlin was helping Chiang Kai-shek's party re-establish its authority in Manchuria. It wasn't known at the time that there had been conflictual relations from the 1930s onwards between the Maoist leadership of the Long March and the Stalinist cadres trained in Moscow. But numerous documents and eyewitness accounts have since shed some light on these conflicts.

As for building the International and its sections, Pablo gradually developed the perspective of generalized entryism into the mass parties – whether Social Democratic (which added nothing new to Trotsky's positions from the 1930s), Stalinist (which was more of an innovation) or even Third World populist and anti-imperialist parties such as the Bolivian MNR. This entryism was described as being *"sui generis"* ("of a special type"), in the sense that sections would maintain an independent, public existence – which usually took the form of publishing a confidential journal or newspaper. But the orientation was extremely controversial given that it committed members to joining parties they had openly fought against for years and which had often subjected them to political persecution and even physical aggression. This was especially the case when dealing with monolithic parties trained in a visceral anti-Trotskyism and lacking even rudimentary features of democratic functioning. It was no surprise that the majority of the French section refused to enter the PCF, considered to be among the most Stalinist parties of the international Communist movement.

The arguments advanced to back this entryist turn were based on the legitimate concern that the FI be "integrated into the real movement of the masses" – in a post-war context where the traditional parties had regained their dominant electoral and trade-union position in the working class. But this quest to be part of the "real movement of the masses" fell within the scope of a long-term strategic outlook founded on the risky forecast of an "imminent war-revolution" in which the Stalinist parties would be forced to shift leftwards in order to defend the non-capitalist social relations on which the power of the Soviet bureaucracy was based.

The Third Congress of the Fourth International was held in 1951, with 74 delegates from 25 countries in attendance. A good chunk of the agenda was taken up by the debate on the nature of the Soviet satellite states. A majority defined them as having become "bureaucratically deformed workers states" from the time new social relations had been imposed, without a revolution from below. However, it was a difficult matter to determine the specific event by which this transformation had taken place. Indeed, this difficulty implied a re-examination of the Russian Revolution itself. Was the decisive factor for revolutionary change the formation of a self-organized political power; or was it the expropriation of the bourgeoisie? Did it reside in the political form of emancipation, or in its social content?

The Congress confirmed the analysis that preparations were underway for a new world war. It highlighted the role played by the arms economy in the recovery of growth. Its Manifesto asserted that the struggle for the defeat of imperialism did not mean a struggle for victory by the Kremlin. It noted that certain Communist Parties had broken away from their absolute subordination to the Soviet Union and had therefore ceased to be strictly speaking Stalinist – even where their internal regime and their relationship to the mass movement remained deeply affected by Stalinism. The Congress distanced itself from Belgrade, whose UN representatives had refused to criticize the American intervention in Korea. It forecast that the threat of war would lead to closer ties between the USSR and China; and it expressed unconditional support for the armed struggles for national liberation underway in Algeria, Cuba, Vietnam and Nicaragua.

In his introductory report to the Congress, Pablo told delegates that the FI's "attachment to the USSR enables us to be in the same camp as the world revolutionary forces opposed to imperialism." Influenced by the Argentinean Trotskyist Posadas, he changed his approach to Latin American populism, rejecting characterizations of it as a form of under-developed fascism. In their response, Bleibtreu and Gibelin took Pablo to task for turning the defence of the USSR into a strategic line on the basis of his speculation about the "centuries of transition". While agreeing with the forecast that a new war was probable, they argued that the room for compromise that existed between imperialism and the Kremlin meant that one could expect a delay of "two or four years" – which must be used to full effect in order to give the revolutionary upsurge the attention it deserved.

Following the Congress, the International leadership applied the policy of entryism *sui generis*. The majority of the French section stuck to its line of adopting a "subsidiary entryism". The International Secretariat then suspended 13 members (representing the majority position in the section) from the central committee of the French section. With five Secretariat members in favour and four against, the measure sparked off a firestorm and simultaneously raised the thorny question of the degree of centralization that should be attached to the FI's foundational notion of "world party". The authoritarian centralism of the statutes was struck down much later, at the Tenth World Congress in 1974 – where it was decided that elected national leaderships could not be removed by an international body. A resolution from the Twelfth World Congress in 1985 further states that it is the sections that join the International and not individual members. This resolution on the "International of sections" provided a modest interpretation of the notion of "world party" and deepened the International's federalist character.

In spite of the political and theoretical importance of the questions debated at the Third Congress, the gathering did not give rise to any major divisions. Following the Congress, however, the crisis in the French section unleashed various centrifugal forces. The split spread across the International in 1952 and 1953 and increased the weight of national factors – which would come to predominate, especially in the current led by Pierre Lambert in France (whose original founders Marcel Bleibtreu, Marcel Gibelin and Michel Lequenne were all excluded by 1955) and by Gerry Healy in Britain. Initially, through its representative on the International Secretariat, the American SWP had supported the positions of the International majority, including the disciplinary measures taken against the majority of the French section. But faced with McCarthyism, and boxed in by liquidationist pressures and isolation from the world movement, SWP leaders took matters into their own hands. The drafting of documents for the Fourth World Congress precipitated a split.

A report submitted by Pablo in early 1952 spelled out his wish that sections should go beyond the stage where they had in practice been reduced to the status of mere propaganda groups. In the immediate post-war period – "rich with revolutionary possibilities" – it was "logical to attempt to carry out essentially independent work." But the Cold War had meant entryism should become a general line: "Attempting to replace the bureaucratic leadership of the masses from the outside with our own independent organizations could isolate us from these masses." This entryism into the mass parties did not pursue the illusory objective of transforming them into revolutionary parties, but rather that of encouraging the development of critical tendencies within them. The danger was not that sections would stay in these parties for too long a time, but rather that they would "move too quickly" and mistake "the movements of a narrow vanguard for the radicalization of the broad mass." In his view, the Third Congress had only begun a necessary reorientation by "breaking down formalistic and schematic doctrinal barriers." It would thereafter be a matter of learning to "start from where the masses themselves start." The draft resolution for the Fourth Congress drove the message home: "We neither can nor want to skip stages [...] We want to merge in action with the movement of the class at its present level, in action and not in program [...] We take the class as it is [...] Form is of little importance [...] " Mass parties became "areas of work". In summary, "the International has been making the biggest gains since it came into being; it is marching almost everywhere with the real movement of the masses, setting itself apart from it only as its revolutionary Marxist conscience." For, "the logic of the international situation is Trotskyist."

This triumphalist rhetoric draws attention to the agonizing struggle that took place between, on the one hand, the desire to be part of the real movement and, on the other, the need to send reassuring propagandistic messages to the converted. While "Pabloism" has often provided a pretext for the airing of groundless accusations, Pablo's approach did indeed reflect a tendency to rely more on the influence of ideas than on the actual relationship of forces, on the role of individuals rather than on the collective, and on looking for political shortcuts rather than on developing a strong organizational culture.

Roughly speaking, the two main international currents formed out of the 1952 split gave expression to two different approaches towards overcoming the movement's isolation. While one side advocated drawing closer to the Stalinist parties, the other side sought refuge in the shadow of Social Democracy, the trade-union bureaucracy, and even Freemasonry in the case of the Lambertists. One pole was established around the International Secretariat; another around the International Committee, whose main member organizations were the American SWP, the Socialist Labour League in Britain, the Internationalist Communist Organization (OCI) in France and Nahuel Moreno's group in Argentina. The split assumed a specific character in Latin America, where the personalities of the two Argentinean leaders -- Juan Posadas (Homero Cristalli) and Nahuel Moreno (Hugo Bressano) – played an important role. Their respective groups had disagreed on the attitude to strike toward the Peronist movement. While the Internationalist Communist Group (GCI) of Posadas advocated working alongside Peronist workers, Moreno's Marxist Workers Group (GOM) characterized Peronism as a semi-fascist movement that sought to crush the workers movement. Neither group had been recognized as the official section at the Second World Congress in 1948. The factional dynamic at play led the Third Congress to recognize the GCI as the official section, with Posadas given the job of establishing a Latin American Bureau. Moreno promptly retaliated by creating his own Latin American

Secretariat. This would entrench the division among Latin American Trotskyists for many years to come.

Less than ten years later, a large majority of the central players in the 1952-1953 split concluded that it had been politically unjustified. A few important lessons can be drawn from the lasting damage caused by the split:

The first lesson concerns the danger for small organizations of splitting over short-term tactical differences rather than questions of principle. The very weakness of the organization means that each of its components is tempted to implement its own ideas without fear of losing much in return.

The second lesson concerns the danger of extrapolating the practical consequences of a theoretical disagreement. As early as 1953, the support given by the International majority to the uprising that year in East Berlin would reveal the limits of its supposed adaptation to Stalinism. Small organizations, which have a very limited scope for practical work, can be tempted to prematurely draw organizational conclusions on the basis of forecasts – instead of basing themselves on the test of major events.

The final lesson is that the relationship between an international organization and its national sections are always delicate. At a national congress, delegates backing a majority position must subsequently shoulder responsibility for the consequences of their decision, even if it means rectifying the position after going through a common experience. This is a basic principle of responsibility and of the reality of political life. On the other hand, in an international organization it is hardly democratic to make French and American rank-and-file members vote on electoral tactics and organizational priorities in Bolivia, and vice-versa. The role of an international organization is to adopt a common position on major world events (without hiding the unavoidable existence of potential minority views) and to give sections the widest autonomy to conduct politics on the national level.

As for "Pabloism", it has been demonized to such an extent as to have become a derogatory term in some quarters. But was "Pabloism" a reality or merely a mythical notion invented out of polemical necessity? By the end of the 1940s, the conditions in which the Fourth International had been created had significantly changed. Its project required redefinition. Pablo was bold enough to shoulder this task. His approach could certainly have led to the pursuit of substitutes and short-cuts, given a context in which the proletariat of the industrialized countries appeared to be further removed from a revolutionary perspective than ever before. Others sought out such substitutes in the Communist movement (as in the case of very marginal groups such as the one around Michèle Mestre in France); while some created "centrist" currents that wavered between reformism and anti-capitalist revolution; and others looked to the anti-colonial revolution (with Pablo himself becoming a close advisor to Makarios in Cyprus and Ben Bella during the first years of the Algerian revolution). A final set of people chose one set of substitutes over another: in France, the Lambertist current buried itself within the bureaucracy of the Force Ouvrière (FO) trade-union confederation; while in Argentina the Moreno current did a 180 degree turn in 1955 and sang the praises of Perón. Most of those claiming to fight this impatience fell into a void of timeless propagandism and dogmatic orthodoxy.

From as far back as the 1950s onwards, Pablo boldly took up questions such as women's liberation, self-management and socialist democracy. His active solidarity with the Algerian revolution (in 1962, he was tried in the Netherlands for counterfeiting money to finance arms production for the FLN) and his work in support of Irish republicans testify to his sense of initiative. Pablo left the Fourth International and launched the International Revolutionary Marxist Tendency in 1965 on the basis of differences over the Sino-Soviet conflict and support for liberation movements in Angola. However, he was keen to rejoin the FI a few years before his death (in 1996), as if to give some continuity to his long life as a political activist by returning to the fold.

6. Entryism, or "where's the exit?"

For Trotskyist organizations, the 1950s were a difficult decade spent in the political wilderness. The gap between the "objective conditions" – still supposedly growing riper by the day – and the persistently defective "subjective factor" continued to grow. However, from 1956 onwards – with the uprisings in Poland and Hungary, on the one hand; and the Algerian war of liberation and the Granma landing in Cuba, on the other – the tide began to turn. It appeared that a convergence between the anti-bureaucratic revolution in the East and the anti-colonial revolution in the South could be in the offing. History was showing signs of a thaw, but life was not necessarily reappearing where one had expected. The working class in the industrialized countries was missing in action. Thus was born the recurring notion of a "detour" – as if there were some norm of historical development, and out of sheer capriciousness reality refused to live up to this standard.

Events nevertheless enabled some of the scattered tribes to see that they were broadly in agreement when it came to providing active support to the Algerian, Cuban and Vietnamese revolutions, and to the anti-bureaucratic uprisings in Eastern Europe. Beginning in the late 1950s, convergence around these questions opened the path to reunification. Contact was restored between the International Secretariat and the International Committee. A joint commission organized the 1963 Reunification Congress (Seventh World Congress), which brought together sections from 26 countries and adopted a resolution entitled "Dynamics of World Revolution Today", which laid down the bases for agreement. The USSR continued to be defined as a bureaucratically degenerated workers state. "In spite of the usurpation of power by a privileged bureaucracy," the Congress re-asserted the need to defend the USSR, while discarding Pablo's questionable formulations. It also explicitly rejected illusions that the Eastern Bloc countries would reform themselves under Khrushchev's leadership. The political lessons of the events in Poland and Hungary helped the Congress define the precise content of the political revolution and the forms that socialist democracy would take in the future. The beginning of the Sino-Soviet split heralded the end of the Stalinist monolith. In spite of the relatively progressive role of the Chinese leadership, their "belated" understanding and critique of Stalinism prevented them from offering an international alternative to the Kremlin bureaucracy.

The Congress highlighted the dynamic of anti-imperialist struggles as demonstrated by the radicalization of the Cuban Revolution in 1961 and 1962, with the defeat of the Bay of Pigs invasion and the Second Declaration of Havana. The expropriation of large property holdings in October 1960 and the deepening of the agrarian reform were greeted as the beginning of a new epoch in the history of the world revolution. They signal the rise of a socialist state under the leadership of a party that had not come out of Stalinism. The Congress saw the trajectory of the 26th of July Movement as a possible model for other movements, while simultaneously asserting the need to "infuse Trotskyist concepts" into the Castroist current emerging in Latin America and Europe.

The Congress rejected the defeatism which manifested itself among the orthodox Communist Parties in the subordination of the class struggle to the struggle between camps. In the midst of the euphoria created by the success of the Sputnik space mission, Khrushchev had promised to catch up to the capitalist world by the end of the century. The orthodox Communist Parties saw the "socialist camp" as the main driver of global progress. The Congress similarly rejected the determinism underlying a Third Worldism (Sartre, Fanon, Sweezy) that despaired of the capacities of the working class and saw the colonial revolution as the only hope for emancipation. Talk of equilibrium between the "three sectors of the world revolution" (the political revolution in the East, the colonial revolution in the South, and the socialist revolution in the industrialized countries) was nevertheless rather superficial. While they could be seen with hindsight as harbingers of May 1968, there was no common measure between the Belgian strikes of 1961, on the one hand, and the Cuban Revolution and Budapest Commune, on the other.

The Congress noted once again the gap between the correctness of the revolutionary movement's ideas and its organizational weakness. Though it proved that the 1953 split had been largely unjustified, the 1963 reunification was incomplete. On the side of the International Committee, Gerry Healy's Socialist Labour League (SLL) in Britain and Pierre Lambert's Internationalist Communist Organization (OCI) in France hardened their sectarian approach to the colonial revolution. Michel Raptis (Pablo) had been blamed for the 1952 crisis and became the bête noire of the International Committee; he left the International in 1965 on the basis of disagreements over Algeria and a refusal to respect the FI's majority positions. Juan Posadas, whose planetary megalomania was degenerating into insanity, had already left in 1962. Though active in solidarity work with the Algerian FLN and within networks such as *Jeune résistance*, where it recruited a new generation of members, the French section was also losing members who supported the *Voie communiste* journal and who were growing increasingly critical of entryism. This included members such as Félix Guattari, Denis Berger, Gabriel Cohn-Bendit and the anthropologist Lucien Sebag.

The 1963 reunification appeared to chart a course that would help the International steer clear of both sectarian temptation and the hunt for shortcuts and substitutes. Its architects agreed not to examine the controversial matter of entryism. Consequently, while the Congress cleared the way for ending this controversial practice, it did so without a balance sheet and without clarity.

Entryism is a catch-all term that evokes a murky universe of manoeuvres and double-dealing; but it actually encompassed a wide array of situations. In a democratic working-class movement, the very idea of entryism is both unknown and meaningless. Before 1914, revolutionary currents existed within reformist organizations. They openly fought for their positions and no one would have thought to label them entryists. Today revolutionary currents with their own public press are active within the Brazilian Workers Party, argue for their positions and run candidates for leadership positions without anyone accusing them of being disloyal. Paradoxically, one of the rare precedents for secretive infiltration was the work of the anarchist Mikhail Bakunin, who organized a secret faction within the First International.

The specific term "entryism" only appeared in the 1930s – specifically with the "French turn" of 1934 and the "American turn", when Trotsky called on small groups from the Left Opposition to join Socialist Parties where left currents were emerging. There was nothing secretive about this "entryism". It was to be carried out "with banners unfurled", in the sense that ideas would be promoted openly by organized currents identified as clearly as the functioning of the parties led by Social Democratic bureaucracies would allow. It was also meant as a short-term tactic.

The entryism carried out in the Communist Parties from 1952-1953 onwards was of another kind. This was so for obvious practical reasons, given that the monolithic character and virulent anti-

Trotskyism of the CPs necessitated a considerable degree of secrecy. But it was also a function of a long-term approach; this brand of entryism was not selected to respond to differentiations already occurring within the mass organizations, but rather on the basis of speculation regarding the inevitability of splits under the impact of the expected war. No timeline could be established for this kind of speculative entryism. When some differentiation did eventually take place within the mass parties, it inevitably involved only small minorities who were quite marginal in relation to the parties' big battalions of party members. The partial breaks with these parties that did occur were never on the scale of the major splits that were expected. Organizations cast in the mould of entryism therefore hesitated to leave with the small forces that were prepared to join them, in the expectation that the big breakthroughs were still to come. In relation to the gains that were hoped for, immediate opportunities always seemed premature and prone to producing disappointing results. This meant that there were no solid criteria for knowing when to end an entryist experience. In this way, the question of withdrawal from the mass parties became a bone of contention as devastating as the original entry; and in several instances the organizations involved split twice. In France, for example, it was even the case that some of the same people – such as David Rousset – who had been against entry into the Socialist Party in 1934 were against withdrawal in 1936.

The long-term entryism initiated in 1952 was presented as the way to stay in touch with the real movement during a period of ebbing fortunes for revolutionary forces. It gave rise to a real sensitivity to manifestations of radicalization, along with an openness to new questions, a sense of initiative – and a desire to shift the terms of debate rather than being merely content to vigorously denounce "treacherous leaders". But being buried inside reformist and Stalinist parties also exacted a high toll. On the one hand, members ended up approaching political life by proxy; instead of defining what they should do within the given relationship of forces, they imagined what the leadership of the mass party would do – if only it were revolutionary. As a result, they entered a world of make-believe in which an exercise in pedagogy came to replace work on improving the relationship of forces. Living as parasites on a foreign body, they gradually lost their own organizational culture, which then became difficult to re-establish. This provided an additional and often unconscious reason to put off the decision to leave the mass party – all the more so since new members had been trained in entryist work and had grown accustomed to playing the role of subordinate internal critics, as opposed to developing their own independent practise. It was risky to make the leap from belonging to an oppositional current within a big party to focusing on building a small independent organization. It is no wonder that so many refused to take this step.

To the entryism of the 1930s and of the 1950s must be added a rather unusual variant; with a grain of salt, it can be called Masonic entryism. Indeed, it was more a matter of infiltrating members, sometimes as sleepers, into political and trade-union apparatuses – and even into state institutions. When it is a matter of manoeuvring to outsmart a repressive apparatus or to avoid professional persecution, such an approach can be considered. But for the Lambertist current, originally established in opposition to entryism, this paradoxically became second nature. In his book *Secrets de jeunesse*, Edwy Plenel draws a convincing portrait of Lionel Jospin as a mole waiting for the revolutionary cataclysm foretold in his organization's catastrophist prophecies. This specific form of entryism ended up weaving a complicated web of duplicity, backscratching and impenetrable collusion. It nurtured a paranoid culture very similar to a police approach to historical events; it poisoned the workers movement rather than undoing the damage wrought by Stalinism. The Lambertist current's perversion of entryism hit new lows when it stopped targeting reformist organizations and began infiltrating revolutionary groups. This practice obliged them to concoct the justification that rival organizations were the most pernicious enemies. One can imagine the calibre of intellectual life spawned by Lambert's cloak-and-dagger approach to party-building.

Having failed to draw a sober balance sheet of entryism, the break in the 1960s was neither clear nor well organized. It took place under the pressure of events and was littered with mishaps and missed opportunities. In Italy, the leadership of the Communist Party was more flexible than in France; critical currents were able to emerge around the *La Sinistra* journal. At the same time, and even before 1968, significant sectors of young people had been drawn into the radical currents that were formed under the impact of the Chinese Cultural Revolution and the Latin American revolution. But these breaches remained marginal compared to the vast opportunities that appeared to exist for those carrying out patient long-term work in a party with more than one million members. The Italian section therefore decided to continue entryism, while the new organizations that emerged out of the youth radicalization largely fell under the influence of Maoism.

In Germany, the section's work was focused primarily on Social Democracy and its youth organization, at a time when the Social Democratic student organization was taking on an oppositional role under the leadership of Rudi Dutschke and breaking outright from Social Democracy. Having missed this favourable moment, following 1968 the section tried to make up for lost time by participating in a unitary project of the critical Left – at a time when it was becoming necessary to fight for clarification between the major currents of the far-Left, and especially in relation to Maoism.

In both Italy and Germany, this abortive exit from entryism had long-lasting effects on the shape of the revolutionary Left. In France, on the other hand, a partial break with entryism took place in 1965 under the impact of the youth radicalization, on the basis of student mobilization in the universities and opposition to the war in Algeria. The crisis in the Union of Communist Students (UEC), the demand for internationalist support for the struggle of the Vietnamese people, and the refusal to vote for François Mitterrand in the first round of the December 1965 presidential elections, led to a split in the Communist youth organizations and the formation in April 1966 of the Revolutionary Communist Youth organization (JCR), forerunner of today's Revolutionary Communist League (LCR). The JCR had about 300 members coming out of the youth radicalization, but was not a fully formed project. Rather, it was produced by force of circumstance and the particular brutality of the Stalinist leadership in France. Even though a huge majority of the JCR's leadership also belonged to the French section of the FI, it was decided that the JCR would not be its youth organization but rather an independent organization. This was a compromise between the creation of an independent organization among young people and the continuation of entryism for the adult organization, which was abandoned in May 1968.

The choice between entryism and an independent orientation cannot be settled simply by answering the question, "Where is the radicalization taking place?" The awakening of political consciousness is an uneven process fed by social experience – in the social and trade-union movement, in the big traditional parties, and in the emergence of new phenomena and formations. There is no single path. The real question is that of finding the base of support that can provide leverage for mobilizing the masses. An entryist orientation is conceivable in conditions of repression or when the hegemonic control of reformist bodies dooms independent organizations to a life of stale propagandism and creeping sectarian necrosis. When the situation is more open and spaces exist for independent political work, there is more to lose from entryism than there is to gain. The revolutionary organization itself runs the danger of becoming dependent on – and internalizing the culture of – the very body that was meant to contribute to its strength. As for the members of the party where entryism is being carried out, entryism nurtures a climate of distrust, rumours and disloyalty – creating a whole host of obstacles to political understanding and possible future convergence.

It should also be noted that members engaged in entryism often tended to mutate into something very different. Subjected to both Newton's law of universal attraction and Darwin's law of adaptation to a given habitat, they were assimilated by the very body they had set out to subvert. Lionel Jospin provides a perfect illustration of this; ever the wily politician, François Mitterrand undoubtedly knew exactly what he was doing when he gambled on his underling's ultimate metamorphosis.

7. "With history nipping at our heels"

In 1965, the coup in Brazil, the American landing in the Dominican Republic, Boumédienne's coup in Algeria, the assassination of Lumumba in the Congo, and the massacre of Communists in Indonesia brought a halt to the colonial revolution. Simultaneously, the war of liberation in Vietnam was entering a new phase with the American escalation and the start of bombing raids into North Vietnam. In the United States, Malcolm X symbolized the evolution of the Black movement while the anti-war movement grew on the campuses. The Tricontinental Conference – and, later, the conferences of the Organization of Latin American Solidarity (OLAS) held in Havana in 1965 and 1967 – appeared to herald a new, socialist stage in the colonial revolution, personified by Che Guevara's presence first in the Congo and then in Bolivia. When he was murdered in October 1967, Che became an entire generation's symbol and role model.

Coming in the midst of this ferment, the year 1968 was seen as confirming "the dialectic of the three sectors of the world revolution" highlighted at the time of the 1963 reunification. The colonial revolution was represented by Vietnam with the Tet offensive, but also by Mexico with the massacre at Tlatelolco, and by Pakistan. The Polish student movement and the Prague Spring testified to the rise of the anti-bureaucratic revolution. With the general strike in France, this time around the European workers movement had also entered the fray. This three-pronged advance filled the youth mobilizations with internationalist fervour. New leaders emerged. The German SDS and the French JCR were the two main organizations behind the conference on internationalist solidarity with the Vietnamese revolution that took place in Berlin in February 1968.

While these years were characterized by the spectacular upheaval among young people, the situation in the working-class movement was more contradictory. France saw the biggest strike in its history. However, though the bureaucratic apparatuses were shaken up by these events, political differentiation within the working-class movement remained very limited. Until 1974, strike activity was far more massive and intense in Italy and Britain than in France. Why did this huge increase in struggle not lead to major breaks from the traditional organizations? Organizations such as the LCR in France, the SWP and Militant in Britain, and Lotta Continua and Avanguardia Operaia in Italy, each had thousands of members in the mid-1970s. Some had daily newspapers and even began to make an electoral breakthrough. Compared to the 1950s and 1960s, the qualitative and quantitative difference was clear; but it was still a matter of marginal developments in relation to the main body of the working-class movement, which remained under the control of reformist and Stalinist leaders.

The year 1968 – which symbolizes a decade of struggle (ending in 1976) – came at the end of a long period of economic expansion (the "post-war boom") and at the beginning of the reversal of the long wave. Debates within the radical Left of the 1960s reflected these overriding features of the period. Some tried to understand the inner workings of "neo-capitalism" (André Gorz). Some examined the potentialities of the new working class (Serge Mallet). Some countered quantitative demands with qualitative ones, and the vision of a one-off revolutionary triumph with "revolutionary reformism" (Lucien Goldmann). Immediately after May 1968, utopian notions of unlimited growth even led some to take a headlong plunge with the slogan "everything now" (the *Vive la Révolution* group in France) and others to speak of the immediate fulfilment of communism thanks to the imminent achievement of abundance (the *Il Manifesto* group in Italy).

There was a huge gap between the heady aspirations of a new vanguard galvanized by faraway revolutions, on the one hand, and the mundane aspirations of the majority of workers with no horizon beyond the reform of the welfare state, on the other. Such a state of affairs lent itself well to ultra-Left flights of fancy. The radical Left had long battled in splendid isolation against theories that spoke of neo-capitalism and the co-optation of the working class; the May events in France and the creeping May in Italy appeared to open up breathtaking prospects and a sudden acceleration of history. Revolution within five or ten years seemed to be a real possibility in Europe, but the resurgent vanguard remained limited to a "small radicalized minority" (as the Berlin students proclaimed). It seemed that showing the lead through unbridled activism might be the way to lessen the contradiction. Just as the guerrilla bases had set the Latin American plains aflame and shaken up traditional forces, it was argued that the boldness of the European vanguards would outflank the conservative habits and functioning of the mainstream Left. The clandestine founding congress of the Ligue Communiste as the French section of the Fourth International, and the Ninth World Congress of the FI itself, took place in the spring of 1969. FI gatherings began to resemble a hall of mirrors in which the separate debates within European and Latin American Trotskyism constantly merged and separated. At the Ninth World Congress, the youthful delegation from France joined forces with the Argentinean and Bolivian representatives to pass the resolution on armed struggle in Latin America.

Under the impact of events, the Congress majority was convinced that the period of political isolation had drawn to a close and that the time had finally come to make the transformation from propaganda International into "combat party". This formulation was taken literally. The shift meant working toward a merger between Trotskyist groupings and the new vanguards, such as currents coming out of the OLAS in Latin America, the Black and student movements in the USA, and the Zengakuren in Japan.

In Latin America, the forward momentum of the Cuban Revolution was in high gear. Régis Debray has called this period a time of "hurried Leninism". He had himself theorized the new course in his 1966 book *Revolution in the Revolution?* In the book, he argued that it no longer made sense to patiently build parties that would get institutionalized and bogged down in routine; the guerrilla forces now revealed the energy that could be drawn on among the masses. Che Guevara personally symbolized this unilateral interpretation of the history of the Cuban Revolution. Experiences of armed struggle multiplied across Latin America – in Argentina, Bolivia, Venezuela, Colombia, Chile, Peru, Uruguay, Guatemala and Nicaragua. Latin American Trotskyist organizations were faced with this new state of affairs. After Posadas left the FI, Nahuel Moreno rejoined the unified International. Having previously burned his fingers due to a sectarian approach towards Peronism at the beginning of the 1950s, he was eager to cast his lot in with the new emerging forces. The Argentinean section undertook preparations for armed struggle. Moreno sent the working-class activist Daniel Pereyra to Peru to handle logistics for Hugo Blanco and lay the groundwork for a peasant insurrection in the La Convención valley. As part of the same orientation, Moreno's organization merged with a group in the tradition of radical populism based primarily among agricultural workers in Tucumán province and led by Mario Roberto Santucho. The plan to initiate armed struggle was one of the main bases of the agreement between the two organizations.

However, in 1967 conditions began to change. The shift was illustrated by Che's assassination in Bolivia, which itself followed upon defeats in the Congo and the Dominican Republic. In Peru, Colombia and Central America, pioneers of the armed struggle fell in combat. Moreno seized upon these reversals and backtracked – provoking a break with Santucho, who felt cheated and then spelled out his own project in a little red book entitled *El Unico Camino* (*The Only Road*). At the Ninth World Congress, Argentina was represented by a divided section, with Santucho's PRT-Combatiente group and Moreno's PRT-La Verdad group. The former was represented by Daniel Pereyra, who had just been freed from a Peruvian prison. The resolution on armed struggle – passed in spite of opposition from the American delegation and Moreno – served more to capture the dynamic of the period that was ending than to anticipate the situation that was beginning to take shape.

"Armed struggle" could not be a strategic orientation in and of itself. In its most general sense, the formula expressed a desire to orientate towards currents linked to the Cuban Revolution, rather than a concrete practical orientation. It could be incorporated into an insurrectional strategic perspective (as portrayed in the classic book *L'insurrection armée* by Hans Neuberg, a collective pseudonym), or into a perspective of protracted war inspired by the Chinese and Vietnamese experiences. In as much as the World Congress resolution provided any detail at all, it placed the armed struggle within the logic of a "protracted civil war on a continental scale." It highlighted the "rural guerrilla movement" as the "main axis for an entire period." It insisted on the fact that in Latin America armed struggle essentially meant guerrilla struggle. This assertion was wide off the mark; rural guerrilla forces had in fact experienced one defeat after another. Neither the experience of peasant self-defence in Peru, nor the prestigious struggle of the Tupamaros in Uruguay could be seen as examples of rural guerrilla movements. When the time came to lay down a strategic project, organizations such as the PRT-Combatiente group, the Chilean MIR and the Sandinistas (following the defeat of their guerrilla movement in Pancasan) adopted a perspective much more along the lines of a protracted people's war – albeit one based on a mythical interpretation of the Vietnamese revolution and the Algerian war of liberation.

While it proved to be wrong, Santucho's project had a rational core. It was a matter of breathing new life into Che Guevara's vision, which could not be properly understood as an attempt to repeat the Cuban experience in Bolivia. Che's most ambitious idea was to establish a kind of base for continental struggle in the region where the borders of Argentina, Peru, Brazil and Chile meet. This is what lay behind the Bolivarian make-up of his guerrilla force and the location that was chosen for the preparatory phase. The PRT-Combatiente group and the Bolivian section were well positioned to play an active role given Tucumán's proximity to the Argentinean border with Bolivia. It also didn't hurt that, though simultaneously subjected to pressures of various sorts from the Cuban government, both groups had received serious military training while on the island.

Santucho took Che's project very seriously and sought to draw all the relevant conclusions. His strategy for protracted war combined national liberation (symbolized by the reference to José Martí) and social emancipation (symbolized by the figure of Che). He considered the Argentinean people to be engaged not only in a struggle against their own military dictators, but also in a war against a probable American intervention (for which the precedent of the Dominican Republic offered a model). Consequently, it was necessary to create an army (the ERP, People's Revolutionary Army), obtain heavy armament, properly finance a war chest, plan the creation of liberated zones and oblige international institutions to recognize a state of war. When this project took shape, differences appeared within the PRT-Combatiente group. A number of important figures with a Trotskyist background had remained in the group – such as Daniel Pereyra, Luis Enrique Pujals (murdered in 1972) and Pedro Bonnet (executed in his cell during the 1972 Trelew prison massacre). The 1969 urban revolts in Córdoba, and the 1972 popular uprising that brought Perón back to power, did not quite fit in with the plan that had been drawn up. Differences also surfaced around international questions. Careful not to ruffle the feathers of the Cuban government, Santucho did not express any criticism of Fidel Castro's accommodating positions on the Soviet intervention in Czechoslovakia.

Between 1969 and 1972, there were a number of splits from the PRT-Combatiente group. Pereyra left to create a small armed propaganda group. The Fracción Roja (Red Faction) – which was from the southern part of Buenos Aires and had adopted dissenting views during Santucho's imprisonment and subsequent escape from the Rawson prison to Chile and Cuba – was also expelled. While the PRT-La Verdad group took advantage of the short-lived democratic opening between 1972 and 1974 to grow in size and strengthen its social base, the PRT-Combatiente group declared itself to be in a state of armed peace with the Peronist police but still in a state of war with the US-backed Argentinean army. Given the vast inequality in armed strength, there could be no doubting the outcome of this declaration of war. About one third of Fracción Roja militants were killed in less than two years. Santucho himself, who had left the FI in 1973, fell in battle in 1976.

The debate on armed struggle grew all the more acrimonious within the Fourth International given that lives were in the balance. Differences around this question became the main motivation for the creation in 1972 of the minority Leninist-Trotskyist Tendency (LTT) – on the initiative of the leadership of the American section and the PRT-La Verdad group (renamed the PST, or Socialist Workers Party). The FI majority retaliated by creating the International Majority Tendency (IMT).

In Europe, the May 1968 general strike in France and the turbulence of the creeping May in Italy revived revolutionary hopes. The 1967 recession signalled the end of both the postwar boom and the belief in a world of unlimited prosperity. For a generation of activists who were as enthusiastic as they were inexperienced, the final slogan bequeathed by Che – "create two, three, many Vietnams" – resonated like an urgent call to action. New acronyms, organizations and leaders arose across most of the continent. These new vanguard forces divided their loyalties between Maoists and Trotskyists; but the influence of Maoism soon receded as the myth of the Cultural Revolution lost its shine.

Trotskyist groups had been substantially strengthened – especially in France and Britain – as these years of effervescence drew to a close, making the transition from student groups to organizations with deeper social roots. In Spain, the Revolutionary Communist League (LCR) was formed in 1971-1972 out of student struggles and protests against the Burgos trial. In Euskadi (Basque Country), the leadership chosen at the ETA's Sixth Assembly and the majority of the organization's political prisoners – who had shifted from nationalism to internationalism under the influence of the Cuban Revolution – joined the Fourth International. Organizations were formed in Sweden, Switzerland and Denmark, not to mention Portugal on the eve of the Carnation Revolution.

In hindsight, one can see that the first half of the 1970s was also characterized by a fevered ultra-Leftism that was fed by constant one-upmanship between revolutionary organizations. To guard against the "enormous condescension of posterity," we must recall the context. For one thing, there had indeed been a huge rise in social struggle up until 1974 – especially in Italy and Britain. For another, in 1973 the entire European Left defined itself strategically in response to the tragedy in Chile. While the Franco dictatorship was in its dying days in Spain, Portugal experienced a genuine revolutionary crisis in 1974-1975. Forms of dual power arose in the summer of 1975 in factories, neighbourhoods and barracks; and in August tanks rode into the streets of Lisbon in support of demonstrators. On the one hand, the Union of the Left in France and the "historic compromise" promoted by Berlinguer in Italy aimed to broaden alliances in a rightward direction in order to protect themselves from a reactionary coup d'état. On the other, the far Left broadly identified with the Chilean MIR and charted a course wherein it would offer critical support to the traditional Left, all the better to prepare for the inevitable confrontations that would follow soon after. By the middle of the 1970s, the far-Left had several thousands of members, and daily newspapers in Italy (*Lotta Continua*, *Il Manifesto*, *Avanguardia Operaia*), France (*Rouge*) and Britain.

The Tenth World Congress of the Fourth International was held at the beginning of 1974, at a crucial turning point between two very different periods. The debate between the International majority and minority focussed on the overall analysis of the situation, on armed struggle in Latin America and revolutionary violence (particularly in relation to ETA's execution of Admiral Carrero Blanco, Franco's presumed successor), on relations with new vanguard forces, and on the united front with the traditional organizations of the working-class movement. Each camp had its own internal discussions. The factional dynamic had created insurmountable obstacles, so the Congress itself looked more like a diplomatic meeting of delegations than a collective gathering for deliberation and debate. Important questions were addressed separately and behind closed doors.

The majority saw the Congress as an opportunity to lay a foundation for the fevered activism of the youthful sections by forecasting an imminent revolutionary crisis in Europe and imagining that the following World Congress would take place in a liberated Barcelona. With the rise of anti-bureaucratic struggles in the East, history would resume from where it had been interrupted in the 1930s by the bureaucratic counter-revolution in the East and the bourgeois counter-revolution in Spain. In April 1974, a few weeks after the Congress, the fall of the Portuguese dictatorship appeared to confirm this forecast. When the British miners' strike culminated in the defeat of the Conservative government, it was described as the precursor of a revolutionary crisis in Britain! It is certainly correct to do everything to transform a genuine possibility into reality – by focussing on forms of self-organization, by encouraging democratic protests in the army, by connecting local struggles to the perspective of a general strike. However, it can prove disastrous when one mistakes a genuine radicalization of struggles for a qualitative change in the relationship of forces within the working-class movement.

The rise of struggles across Europe did indeed lead to the fall of the dictatorships in Greece, Portugal and Spain; and social movements did partially escape the grip of the traditional Left apparatuses. But the traditional Left still held the reins of the political situation. In France, the united Left retook the initiative in 1972. In Italy, the Communist Party achieved its best ever electoral results in 1976. The global recession of 1973-1974 signalled a reversal of the economic situation; and the reining in of the Portuguese revolution in the autumn of 1975 was a political turning point. The reappearance of mass unemployment, the crisis in certain industrial sectors, and the conciliatory approach of reformist leaders combined to defuse a socially explosive situation. In Spain, the Moncloa Pact and the legitimization of the monarchy paved the way for an orderly transition out of the Franco period. In Italy, the historic compromise gave Christian Democracy a reprieve. In Britain, Labour's failure set the stage for Thatcherism. In short, a new order took shape between 1975 and 1978. Kept on tenterhooks by the prospect of an election win for the Left in 1978, France took note of this shift somewhat belatedly – with the breakdown of Left unity in 1977 and the impact of an initial round of austerity measures.

Simultaneously, Latin America was experiencing a retreat of struggle in the Southern Cone (following the coups in Bolivia, Uruguay and Chile in 1973, and Argentina in 1975). The Chilean experience showed that the heroism of a determined minority is not enough to "outflank the apparatuses" when their control over significant sectors of the mass movement has not been broken beforehand. A strategic reorientation had begun.

On the opposite side of the planet, the peoples of Indochina had become symbols for anti-imperialist struggles the world over; and the American debacle in Saigon appeared to herald a new era for oppressed peoples. However, disillusionment quickly set in as news began to arrive of the tragedy in Cambodia and of the armed conflicts between Vietnam and Cambodia and then China and Vietnam.

As segments of the revolutionary Left – especially in Italy and to a lesser extent in Germany and Portugal – went dangerously astray into a fetishization of symbolic violence carried out by tiny groups, it was clear the time had come to adopt an attitude of "impatience in slow motion" and to develop a revolutionary project for the long haul. In the event, the Eleventh World Congress was not a triumphant gathering in Barcelona; rather, it was a discreet affair in Italy. The main players in ten years of factional debates were in a state of exhaustion. Tendencies and factions were dissolved for the most part in 1977 and preparatory work for the Congress led to a cessation of hostilities and a compromise between American and European Trotskyists. For his part, Moreno formed the Bolshevik Faction. The leaders of the former majority and those of the American SWP agreed on an agenda that prioritized programmatic renewal (with the adoption of important resolutions on socialist democracy and on women's liberation) and organizational measures (with a wrenching effort aimed at getting rank-and-file members into industrial jobs). The overall logic of the plan was based on the idea that, with the ebbing of the colonial revolution, a long historical detour was coming to an end. The world revolution's centre of gravity was moving back to the industrialized countries; as a result, it would once again take on its "classical" urban, insurrectionary forms. Consequently, the priorities became unification of the international Trotskyist movement (especially in France and Brazil) and the gathering together of the tribes in the diaspora. In 1978, negotiations to this end began between the United Secretariat and the leaders of the Organizing Committee for the Reconstruction of the Fourth International (OCRFI), whose main leader was Pierre Lambert.

Once again, events intervened to disrupt the outlook on which preparations for the upcoming World Congress had been based. The proposed orientation banked on the exhaustion of the colonial revolution and the return of the revolutionary epicentre to the industrialized countries. But the capitalist counter-offensive of the Thatcher-Reagan years had begun and world headlines were dominated by events in Iran and Central America – especially by the Sandinista revolution of July 1979 in Nicaragua. Even before these developments, the nuptials to be performed at the World Congress were prompted more by cold logic than romantic passion; in the new context, the event was bound to be an even more sullen affair than expected. No one's heart was in it. Lambert and Moreno each thought the time was ripe to get their revenge for past frustration by delivering a deathblow to the international organization whose permanent or intermittent dissidents they had been for the better part of thirty years. They seized upon the opportunity thrown up by the Nicaraguan revolution and accused the United Secretariat of having capitulated to the petty-bourgeois Sandinista leadership by refusing to build a hard-line Trotskyist organization in Nicaragua. In the autumn of 1979, pre-empting the World Congress called for early 1980, Moreno's Bolshevik Faction and the Leninist-Trotskyist Tendency (LTT) – essentially the product of Lambertist entryism into the French section, steered by Jean-Christophe Cambadélis and led by Daniel Gluckstein and Christian Phéline – quit the International to create a joint committee with the OCRFI. Their "open world conference" in December 1980 had all the trappings of a founding convention for a new International – with the reports and resolutions aimed at laying down the boundaries between "orthodox Trotskyism" and "liquidationist revisionism".

As the representative of the United Secretariat pointed out in his remarks, the question of Central America – the pretext for this new split – had still not even been addressed by the fifth day of the conference. And yet the preparatory texts for the gathering had characterized the FI's sections' support for the Central American revolution as "the worst betrayal in the history of Trotskyism," comparable to the failure of the Third International at the time of the Chinese revolution of 1927, the German defeat in 1933 and the Spanish Civil War. Here we have a typical example of a sect that is incapable of rising to the major events of the day and that shrinks the world down to its own minute scale. The tragedies of the past are replayed as grotesque farces where pathetic little runts behave as if they were the giants of yesteryear. However ridiculous this shadow theatre may appear, it confirmed one constant feature in the history of Trotskyist organizations: derisory though they may be, their rifts and splits echo the great events defining an era.

8. Changing times

With the capitalist counter-offensive, the Reagan administration's new arms race, the American "low intensity" war in Central America, and Britain's expeditionary force to the Malvinas-Falklands Islands (foreshadowing a new round of imperialist intervention), the beginning of the 1980s signalled a radical change over the previous decade. The Soviet Union had sunk into the deep stagnation of the Brezhnev period. The international working-class movement was being thrown onto the defensive on nearly every front. This reversal opened the way for major social-movement defeats – such as the defeat of the British miners' strike in 1984, the failure of the Italian movement in defence of wage indexation in 1985, and trade-union defeats in the USA and Japan during the same period. In France, the austerity turn sealed the Socialist Party's conversion to social-liberalism.

Still, despite this right-wing counter-offensive, signs of renewal were appearing – especially in Brazil with the foundation in 1979 of the Workers Party (PT), which would become one of the country's main political organizations within a decade; and in South Korea, with the huge student mobilizations and formation of new trade unions. Nevertheless, the Nicaraguan revolution – which had fired hopes for a revival of the Latin American revolution – failed to spread to El Salvador and Guatemala. It had been contained by the strategy of counter-insurgency implemented with Israeli and Taiwanese assistance, and by the so-called "low intensity" war waged by the Americans. In the Southern Cone, the transition away from dictatorship was relatively well handled by the ruling classes of Brazil, Argentina, Uruguay and Chile, where social movements were still reeling from the blows endured under the military heel. The last major Bolivian miners' strike (in 1985) brought to a close the period inaugurated by the Bolivian revolution of 1952. The fraudulent victory of Salinas de Gortari against Cuauhtémoc Cárdenas in the Mexican elections of 1988 was a highly symbolic event; it cleared the way for the dismantling of the populist welfare state and initiated a wave of major neoliberal reforms: privatization, agrarian counter-reform, and the signing of a free-trade agreement with the USA and Canada.

At the beginning of the 1980s, a rejuvenated and highly internationalized Fourth International collective leadership team – from the USA, Mexico, Spain, Sweden, Japan, Belgium, Italy, Switzerland, Australia, Britain and France – initiated a wide range of organizational projects. These included the establishment of a permanent international leadership school, an overhaul of the press, support for the creation of youth organizations, and the setting up of continental coordinating bodies. However, differences reignited by the revolution in Central America showed that the FI was running out of steam.

A product of the December 1980 Open World Conference, the International Committee lasted only a few short months. Its unity had been based on opposition to the "United Secretariat liquidationists" and lacked a solid foundation. True to his brand of pragmatic manoeuvring, Lambert steered clear of core political debates – at a time when the Nicaraguan revolution was reviving old debates regarding the characterization of the Chinese, Yugoslav and Cuban revolutions and their political leadership. For his part, Moreno settled the matter by declaring that the October Revolution had been the only authentic social revolution and that the post-war period had only experienced "February revolutions" with no genuine self-organization among the masses; these revolutions had nonetheless been "categorically socialist", he argued, inasmuch as they had dismantled the existing state apparatus. Moreno presented these theoretical gymnastics in a more systematic way in a book that appeared under the pen name Dariush Karim. The book differentiated a stage of confrontation with imperialism from a stage of socialist construction strictly speaking. This approach sacrificed principles of socialist democracy to *realpolitik* and ultimately diminished the importance of the fight against bureaucracy during the anti-imperialist stage.

Behind the outward show of unity at the Eleventh Congress against the split orchestrated by Moreno and Lambert, cracks began to form within the International majority. The disagreements concerned controversial questions such as the unity of the Trotskyist movement and the "turn to industry", but also unresolved debates reignited by developments in Central America and Poland. Differences revolved yet again around the lag between the revolutionary act of seizing power and the transformation of the relations of production. As 1979 drew to a close, new differences appeared following the entry of Soviet troops into Afghanistan purportedly to defend the secular government against reactionary tribal and religious forces supported by the Pakistani dictatorship.

Besieged by the Cold War mood of the Reagan era, the American SWP opted to support the Soviet intervention. Adopting a more cautious stance, the United Secretariat majority condemned the intervention as being guided primarily by the geostrategic interests of the bureaucracy; but it did not demand the withdrawal of Soviet troops, arguing that the internationalization of the conflict had set secular progressive forces supported by the Soviet Union against reactionary religious forces supported and armed by the United States. A minority around Tariq Ali, Gilbert Achcar and Michel Lequenne took the soundest position – arguing that the Soviet intervention would only cloud the meaning of anti-imperialist struggle and bolster the most reactionary religious and nationalist forces. They demanded the immediate withdrawal of Soviet troops and advocated support for the most progressive elements of the Afghan resistance. In 1982, the International adopted a self-critical resolution along the lines of this position. This fumbling approach was an example of the difficulty the FI was having in relation to new armed confrontations – such as the Malvinas/Falklands conflict and the war between Iran and Iraq – that highlighted the centrifugal dynamics of the new world situation.

And yet, on the eve of the 1980s, developments such as Solidarnosc's anti-bureaucratic struggle in Poland and the rise of the revolution in Central America seemed to lend themselves to a reading of the world situation using updated models of political revolution and permanent revolution. This became the focus of debates leading up to the Twelfth World Congress in 1985. The American SWP and Australian SWP deepened their rapprochement with the Castro leadership in Cuba and revised their traditionally orthodox outlook in harmony with this new orientation. In a 1983 essay entitled "Their Trotsky and Ours", Jack Barnes left no room for doubt: "The change I am proposing is one of the most important ones since the founding of our movement." He argued that the theory of permanent revolution was "an obstacle to reviving the tradition of Marx, Lenin and the first congresses of the Communist International." Trotsky's return to the ultraleft demons of his youth, he added, had cut the Fourth International off from the real historical movement. This was a selective embrace of a brand of Trotskyism purged of the struggle against Stalinism; it enabled Barnes to erase references to the anti-bureaucratic revolution and, on the sly, go back to the position of promoting the reform path in the countries of the Soviet bloc. When the SWP relegated support to the Polish uprising to the background – on the pretext that it might weaken the socialist camp just as Reagan was embarking on a new

Cold War – it confirmed the organization's new turn. The Barnes essay focussed unilaterally on the fact that defence of the Soviet workers state had proven "vital to the extension of the world socialist revolution." He conveniently ignored the cost of the Soviet policy of peaceful coexistence for colonial peoples and the workers of Western Europe; and said nothing about the Greek, Spanish, Indonesian and Chilean tragedies – let alone the price paid by the Chinese, Cubans and Vietnamese for the conditional assistance of their Soviet big brother.

The SWP comrades had always claimed to be the standard-bearers of Trotskyist orthodoxy. That they should find themselves so far adrift was a sure sign of demoralization and the replacement of the class struggle by the struggle between camps and states. The SWP turn seemed all the more unfounded in that – from the OLAS conference onwards – experiences in Latin America and elsewhere had actually prompted a critical review of the stagist strategies of the Stalinist period and called attention to the dissenting strategic lineage shared by such figures as José Carlos Mariátegui from Peru, Antonio Mella from Cuba, Farabundo Martí from El Salvador, and Augusto César Sandino and Carlos Fonseca Amador from Nicaragua. Similarly, the demands of the Polish movement and the Solidarnosc congress of 1980 – captured in the slogan "Give us back our factories!" – actually provided a striking defence and illustration of the strategy of political revolution in the Soviet bloc.

The Australian SWP were more interested in engaging with political developments in their country and weren't as concerned as the leaders of the American section with matters of programmatic heritage. Australian delegates to the Thirteenth World Congress candidly told the gathering that permanent revolution was a "useless fetish" that had led to the sectarian degeneration of the International and to "an overestimation of the role of the political revolution against the castes in power in the bureaucratic socialist states." The Australian delegates were so candid, in fact, that they went so far as to justify the Stalinist repression against Vietnamese Trotskyists – granting only the belated self-criticism of the Vietnamese Communist Party itself, according to which the (anti-Trotskyist) violence had been "excessive relative to the situation."

The majority resolutions for the Twelfth World Congress stressed that the crisis of the international revolutionary leadership could no longer be posed in the same terms as in the 1930s. It was no longer a matter of providing alternative leadership to an international working-class movement bathed in the revolutionary culture of the period opened up by the Russian Revolution. A lot of water had flown under the bridge since that time. That tradition had been destroyed during the long night of Stalinism and by Social Democracy's embrace of the capitalist order. A worldwide renewal of trade-unionism and working-class politics was now on the agenda. It was therefore a matter of plunging into the uneven and prolonged process of rebuilding. The Fourth International could play an irreplaceable role in this process – on the condition that it not see itself as the mythical "World Party" of socialist revolution. "Failing world-shaking events powerful enough to upset the relationship of forces between the classes and cause a general realignment of political forces, the recomposition of the international workers movement will remain slow, uneven and extremely differentiated [...] The time now is neither to abstractly proclaim a mass International nor to search out shortcuts towards that end. We stand now merely at the beginning of profound and lasting transformations in the workers movement. We should approach them by a combination of building the Fourth International as it is and collaborating with the vanguard forces evolving in the different countries and continents." This was an open-ended approach that, however, did not make a clean slate of history; there was no question of scrapping the movement's programmatic heritage – whether around the struggle against bureaucratic totalitarianism or the logic of permanent revolution.

The anticipated major events were not a long time coming – with the overthrow of bureaucratic regimes in 1989, German reunification, and the disintegration of the Soviet Union in 1991. This brought an end to what historians came to call "the short twentieth century" – extending from the First World War and the Russian Revolution through to the collapse of bureaucratic totalitarianism. Far from giving rise to renewed hope and a new project, these events were rather more in the nature of creative destruction – a necessary process of negation and decomposition rather than of recomposition. Following the turning point of 1989-1991, the dynamic of capitalist restoration won the day in the East, with little in the way of popular mobilization in defence of the supposedly workers states. There were no signs of political revolution tending towards workers self-management, and not even the emergence of significant currents advocating a revival of the revolutionary tradition. Meanwhile, the Brazilian PT came close to winning the 1989 presidential elections, the Sandinistas lost the 1990 elections in Nicaragua, and in El Salvador the FMLN laid down its arms after leading a number of failed insurrections. In Cuba, the 1989 trial and execution of General Arnaldo Ochoa – in a Moscow-style show trial – revealed the scale of bureaucratic decay within the country's increasingly dictatorial regime.

For a minority within the FI, however, the fall of Stalinist despotism and the good news that blew in on the East Wind were a cause for celebration with copious amounts of champagne. The FI majority responded along Spinozian lines: neither laughing nor crying, but trying to understand. There was nothing to lament – on the contrary – about the fall of these regimes. Their function since the 1930s had been to preserve a world order created through negotiation with the imperialist powers, and to smother working-class movements in their own countries. Their collapse was the epilogue of a bureaucratic counter-revolution completed long before. In the context of the 1980s, though, their fall did not benefit the people but rather the rulers, the rich and bureaucrats transformed into mafia-style capitalists. Champagne? Sure, but with a strong dose of Alka Seltzer as a chaser. The bureaucratic dictatorships had indeed fallen under the pressure of popular movements and velvet revolutions in East Germany, Czechoslovakia, Poland and Romania; but they had also fallen under the pressure of the world market and the imperialist-initiated arms race. The iron grip of the bureaucracy had lasted more than 50 years in these countries; it had shattered political traditions, atomized the proletariat, destroyed public life and demolished civil society. Aspirations for reform and political revolution had indeed appeared at the time of the 1956 uprisings in Hungary and Poland, during the Czechoslovak spring of 1968, and in the working-class struggles of 1976 and 1980 in Poland. But the appearance of Solidarnosc marked the end of an old cycle rather than the beginning of a new one. A far cry from Khrushchev's promise to catch up to and overtake capitalism, the Soviet Union had been sinking into a deep stagnation from the mid-1970s onwards. The Soviet regime was going senile, life expectancy was beginning to decrease, and the economy was suffocating under the controls and waste of a petrified bureaucracy. Unlike what had occurred in the 1960s, the working-class movement in the West – thrown on to the defensive by neoliberal reforms – was unable to exert even the slightest attraction on the protest movements in the East. Russian, Polish and East German workers dreamed of a Swedish standard of living. In reality, the implacable law of uneven and combined development condemned them to a subordinate role in the world market, to a massive decline in their living conditions, and to political instability – hovering between truncated democratization and authoritarian backsliding, bearing a greater resemblance to countries of the Third World than to "Western democracies".

These momentous developments obviously called into question the very raison d'être of organizations with roots in Trotskyism. In their own way, the leaders of the American SWP had anticipated the events in Eastern Europe – opting to quietly leave the International with the prospect of "merging with the Castroist current." The Australian SWP had preceded them along this path with its attempts to link up with new forms of radicalization, particularly in Asia and Oceania. Conversely, a minority of the French section claimed that the fall of the bureaucratic dictatorships heralded an imminent political revolution. The Thirteenth World Congress met in January 1991, on the eve of the Gulf War and the implosion of the Soviet Union. The majority resolution focussed on the contradiction between this euphoric outlook and the fact that the orthodox Trotskyism championed by this current was, by its own admission, holed up and under siege in a few residual holy places such as Paris and San Francisco. If the situation was as wonderful as they claimed, why did they represent such a small minority within organizations that were themselves rather marginal? The position was untenable; and the minority was hit hard by the disillusionment that soon followed. Most of the French supporters of the Congress minority position promptly joined the Socialist Party, led by Gérard Filoche and Daniel Assouline. This confirmed the old rule that the most ostentatious displays of orthodoxy sometimes set the stage for the most spectacular capitulations. With some time lag, the French minority was following the move to the Socialist Party initiated at the beginning of the 1980s by Julien Dray, Henri Weber, Harlem Désir and Pierre Moscovici from the LCR; and by Jean-Luc Mélanchon, Jean-Christophe Cambadélis and 400 other members of the Lambertist OCI. This embrace of the Socialist Party reflected the May 68 generation's newfound appetite for administrative realism and positions of power – which Mitterrand exploited masterfully through his paternalistic sponsorship of the anti-racist campaigning group SOS Racisme. This return to the old Socialist homestead – of which Léon Blum had declared himself caretaker at the Tours Congress in 1920 – was also a way of bidding farewell to the proletariat and the lyrical illusions of the post-68 period. Lionel Jospin's silent transformation was part of this overall redeployment.

9. Conclusion or continuation

As the "short twentieth century" drew to a close, so too did a cycle in the history of the working-class movement. A new chapter is just now beginning. Trotskyists were the first to fight Stalinism, in the name of revolutionary Marxism. But does the history of Trotskyism now end, along with that of Stalinism? Will some of the currents that come out of this experience successfully redeploy their experience and memory in a new context whose contours are just beginning to take shape? Will they be able to harness their experience to enrich the re-emerging social movements? Will they be able to provide a bridge between the lessons of the past and the challenges of the future? The answer cannot be known beforehand; it depends on future struggles.

Of the different branches that grew out of Trotskyism's origins, the Fourth International and the International Socialism current (the British SWP's international current) are the most significant – given their presence in certain key countries and their actual international weight. Their groups and sections are generally very active in the international movement against capitalist globalization and imperialist war, and in the renewal of social movements. They are often involved in national regroupments with currents from the Communist Party tradition, radical ecology and revolutionary feminism. The Moreno and Lambert tendencies have been weakened and by and large only exert influence on a national or regional level. The Militant tendency from Britain has split into various groupings. In France, Lutte Ouvrière (LO) received more than five percent of votes in the 1995 presidential elections and often rates better in opinion polls than the Communist Party candidate; but LO is a phenomenon specific to France, where taken together the far-Left of Trotskyist extraction gets between 5.5 percent and 12 percent (in some municipalities) of votes cast, depending on the type of election.

How can Trotskyists enter the new century without renouncing their past or slipping into sectarianism? They will have to update their theory and practice – and challenge a vision of history linked to the teratological vocabulary of "degeneration" and other "monstrosities" that presupposes a standard, unilinear course of historical progress.

This essay stops on the threshold of the 21st century. But the march of world events itself does not. The times are more convulsive and violent than ever before. It is no longer merely a crisis of growth, but a full-blown crisis of a civilization in its twilight years. The social relations of human beings between themselves – and the human relationship with the natural conditions of our species' reproduction – cannot be reduced to the short-sighted arbitrations of the markets and the generalized poverty of market measurements. When they declare that "the world is not for sale," demonstrators against imperialist globalization in Seattle and Genoa – but also in Porto Alegre (the symbolic city where the Trotskyist leftwing of the Workers Party has played a decisive role over the last 20 years) – raise the question of what we want for humanity and what kind of world we wish to live in. If the world should not be a commodity, what should it be? And what exactly are our plans for this world?

The collapse of "actually non-existent socialism" has freed the new generation from anti-models that paralyzed the imagination and compromised the very idea of communism. But the alternative to Capital's barbarism will not take shape without a thoroughgoing balance sheet of the terrible century that has just ended. In this sense, at least, a certain type of Trotskyism – or a certain spirit of Trotskyism in all its variants – is not outmoded. Its instruction-deficient legacy is certainly insufficient; but it is nonetheless necessary for those who wish to unravel the association between Stalinism and communism, to free the living from the weight of the dead, and to turn the page on the disillusions of the past.

Postscript to the Italian edition

The original French edition of this small book on Trotskyism was published in February 2002. Two months later, the April 2002 presidential elections saw the socialist candidate eliminated in the first round. The second round was a mug's game between outgoing president Jacques Chirac and far-Right candidate Jean-Marie Le Pen. The trauma caused by this unexpected turn of events somewhat overshadowed another major feature of the election results: for the first time, two candidates associated with Trotskyism – Arlette Laguiller from Lutte Ouvrière and Olivier Besancenot from the LCR – came out ahead of the Communist Party (PCF) candidate. Together they received 10 percent of the vote, as opposed to 3.5 percent for the PCF. This peculiarity of the French scene did not fail to attract the attention of journalists and political analysts.

And yet France is not an exception. Some thought that political currents from the historical tradition of Trotskyism were doomed to wither and fade away. After all, the argument went, their role as critics of Stalinism had evaporated following the collapse of the Berlin Wall and the implosion of the Soviet Union. But these currents have survived. Of course, they have transformed themselves – but they have done so without abandoning their heritage. The end of the twentieth century also marked the end of the historical cycle inaugurated by the First World War and the Russian Revolution. However, the new century which began under the ashes of the Twin Towers of New York has not started from zero; nor can we make a clean sweep of the past. We always start again in the middle, as Gilles Deleuze would say. Following the failure of "real socialism", Louis Althusser mourned the destruction of "a world of thought". In our case, our world of thought requires critical examination, but it has neither been buried under the rubble of the Berlin Wall nor swallowed up by the Gulag. It survives as a thread of understanding essential for deciphering the riddles of the present.

Re-energized by the emergence of the global justice movement in 1999, Trotskyism (or at least some of its currents) has survived the bureaucratic debacle. It has even made new progress in new geographic areas – particularly in Asia, and more modestly in Africa and the Arab world. It has also made a fragile comeback in Russia, Ukraine and Eastern Europe.

This resurgence can be explained easily enough.

For one thing, neo-liberal globalization has generated a need not only for international solidarity but also for a common understanding of the events and requirements of the present context – whether in response to global environmental challenges, in opposition to the global war without end, or in the fight against multinationals and social dumping. But now there are effectively no remaining "socialist motherlands" in a position to provide logistical support (usually on unfavourable terms) and serve as a base for these movements. The demise of the Soviet Union, and China's conversion to capitalism, has freed the currents of revolutionary Marxism from the orthodoxies that held them in their grip for so long. Likewise, a new form of active internationalism has been freed from the stranglehold of state and diplomatic interests.

For another, today's new revolutionaries feel a pressing need to gain a thorough understanding of the failures of the past and the lessons for the future – not out of academic curiosity, but to find their bearings in these sombre times. Having failed to understand the difference between the Russian Revolution and the bureaucratic counter-revolution, and between Bolshevism and Stalinism, many erstwhile doctrinaire "communists" have become zealous Social Democrats – while others have even become soldiers in the West's anti-totalitarian crusade.

Lastly, while Trotskyists have experienced the defeats of the broader working-class movement and suffered their consequences, they have not experienced the political and moral bankruptcy of the big Left parties. That is why they have at least earned the right to start again and to continue on – in the manner of those social revolutions which Marx said *"criticize themselves constantly, interrupt themselves continually in their course, come back to the apparently accomplished in order to begin it afresh, deride with unmerciful thoroughness the inadequacies, weaknesses and paltriness of their first attempts."* While Trotskyists are not in a position to single-handedly fill the vacuum created by the collapse of the Stalinist parties and the conversion of Social Democrats into moderate neoliberals, they can enrich new generations of activists with the wealth of their experience.

Indeed, it is now that the "baggage of exodus" – lugged for many long years around a "planet without a visa"– has proven to be invaluable.

There has been an uneven but real upturn in social struggle since the beginning of the new century; the Bolivarian revolution in Latin America faces a number of challenges; and the illusion that the new social movements are all that is required to meet the challenges of capitalist globalization has been discredited. Such developments have placed the strategic question of power back on the agenda, resurrecting it from the dark and dusty corners where it had languished since the end of the 1970s. The forces involved in the anti-globalization movement and social forums are at a crossroads. For starters, the most politically aware among them must make the leap from ideological condemnation of neo-liberalism to political anti-capitalism. Failing this, they are doomed to embrace the illusory *realpolitik* of participation in neoliberal governments such as the ones led by Lula in Brazil and Prodi in Italy. The link between social movement and political representation must be firmly established; when it is not, the example of Rifondazione Comunista in Italy has shown how short the path can be from spouting radical social-movement rhetoric to occupying an utterly servile position within a governmental alliance.

On a symbolic level, it says a great deal about our political ethics that two of our comrades have been sacrificed by their parties on the altar of class collaboration. Senator Heloisa Helena was expelled from the Brazilian Workers Party (PT) in 2003 for refusing to support a neo-liberal reform of the pension system. In striking this stance, she was merely sticking to the positions adopted at the PT's most recent party congress. In Italy, Senator Franco Turigliatto was expelled from Rifondazione Comunista in 2006 for refusing to vote in favour of an imperial military expedition to Afghanistan. These comrades were worthy of their elders who, in the far more tragic circumstances of the Stalinist show trials, were virtually alone in refusing to "confess". In their memoirs, Leopold Trepper and David Rousset say that this was because the Trotskyists did not renounce their political positions and knew exactly what they were being accused of. In the life of a revolutionary, some principles are worth a great deal more than a seat in parliament.

By avidly participating in the methodical demolition of the welfare state, European Social Democracy has helped to saw off the branch on which it was perched. Blairite and won over to social-liberalism, its strategy now consists of forming centre-Left coalitions and dutifully managing capitalist globalization with an inhuman face. The communist parties that had tied their fate to the Soviet bureaucracy have almost all been swept away by its downfall. Having long ago ceased to be revolutionary, they have been doomed to playing the role of second fiddle to Social Democracy; and to being subjected to pressure on their left from the newly resurgent forces of the revolutionary Left.

The renewal of social struggle has opened up a space to the left of the traditional governing parties of the Left. But it isn't an empty space that one can simply occupy. It's a force field, criss-crossed by projects that while sometimes in their infancy are often contradictory with one another. In the 2007 French presidential elections, the LCR's Olivier Besancenot was the only one among the candidates of the non-social democratic Left to better his 2002 results – with more than four percent (1.5 million) of votes. This was not only because he is a talented representative of a generation of rebellious young workers, but also because he placed the dire socio-economic situation at the heart of his campaign, advocated unity in struggle while asserting intransigent independence in relation to the Socialist Party (PS) and prospects of a PS-led government coalition, and framed the day-to-day struggle within a medium-term historical perspective.

Whether in England with Respect, in Portugal with the Left Bloc, in Italy with Sinistra Critica, in Denmark with the Red Green Alliance, or in Turkey with the ÖDP, organizations and activists from the Trotskyist tradition are participating in a non-sectarian way – but with all their convictions intact – to the recomposition now underway. They are also part of the revival of the revolutionary Left in Spain, Germany and Eastern Europe.

One chapter has ended. A new one is just beginning.

Filling the pages of this new chapter will require clarity, courage and a great deal of hurried patience.

May 2007

Bibliography

Books and essays

Alexander, David. *Trotskyism in Latin America*. Stanford: Hoover Institution Press, 1973.

Barta (Albert A. Mathieu). *La Lutte de Classes*, Vol. 1, Nos. 1 to 49. October 1942-July 1945. Reprint of selected articles. Paris: La Brèche, 1992.

Bensaïd, Daniel. *The Formative Years of the Fourth International (1933-1938)*. Amsterdam: IIRE Notebooks for Study and Research No. 9, 1988.

---. Intervention on behalf of the United Secretariat of the Fourth International at the December 1980 Open World Conference, special supplement to *International Viewpoint*.

Bornstein, Sam and Al Richardson. *War and the International: a history of the Trotskyist movement in Britain 1937-1949*. London: Socialist Platform, 1986.

Breitman, George. *The Rocky Road to the Fourth International, 1933-1938*. New York: Pathfinder Press, 1979.

Breitman, George, Paul Leblanc and Alan Wald. *Trotskyism in the United States: historical essays and reconsiderations*. Atlantic Highlands, N.J.: Humanities Press, 1996.

Broué, Pierre. *Trotsky*. Paris: Fayard, 1988.

Callinicos, Alex. *Trotskyism*. Buckingham: Open University Press, 1990.

Calvès, André. *Sans bottes ni médailles. Un trotskyste breton dans la guerre*. Paris: La Brèche, 1984.

Campinchi, Philippe. *Les Lambertistes, un courant trotskyste français*. Paris: Balland, 2000.

Cannon, James. *The History of American Trotskyism*. New York: Pioneer Publishers, 1944.

Chaolin, Zheng. "Chen Duxiu and the Trotskyists." *China's urban revolutionaries: explorations in the history of Chinese Trotskyism, 1921-1952*. Ed. Gregor Benton. Atlantic Highlands, N.J.: Humanities Press, 1996.

Claudín, Fernando. *The Communist Movement: from Comintern to Cominform*. Translated by Francis MacDonagh. 2 vols. New York: Monthly Review Press, 1975.

Castoriadis, Cornelius. *La société bureaucratique*. Paris: UGE, 1973.

Coggiola, Osvaldo. Historia del trotskismo argentino (1929-1960), Buenos Aires: CEAL, 1985.

---. "The History of Argentine Trotskyism." *Revolutionary History* Vol. 2, No. 2, Summer 1989.

Copfermann, Émile. *David Rousset: une vie dans le siècle*. Paris: Plon, 1991.

Cliff, Tony. *State Capitalism in Russia*. London: Bookmarks, 1988.

---. *Trotskyism after Trotsky: the origins of the International Socialists*. London: Bookmarks, 1999.

--- et al. *The Fourth International, Stalinism, and the Origins of the International Socalists*. London: Pluto, 1971.

Craipeau, Yvan. *Le mouvement trotskyste en France*. Paris: Syros, 1972.

Deutscher, Isaac. *The Prophet Armed – Trotsky, 1879-1921*. London: Oxford University Press, 1954.

---. *The Prophet Unarmed – Trotsky, 1921-1929*. London: Oxford University Press, 1959.

---. *The Prophet Outcast – Trotsky, 1929-1940*. London: Oxford University Press, 1963.

Drucker, Peter. *Max Shachtman and His Left: A Socialist's Odyssey through the "American Century"*. Atlantic Highlands N.J.: Humanities Press, 1994.

Essel, André. *Je voulais changer le monde: mémoire*. Paris: Mémoire du livre, 2001.

Fanxi, Wang. *Chinese revolutionary: memoirs, 1919-1949*. Translated by Gregor Benton. Oxford: Oxford University Press, 1980.

Fourrier, Jules. *Graine rouge*. Paris: La Brèche, 1983.

Frank, Pierre. *The Fourth International: the long march of the Trotskyists*. Translated by Ruth Schein. London: Ink Links, 1979.

Lequenne, Michel. "Notes sur notre histoire." *Critique Communiste* 148 and 149 (1997).

Lewin, Moshe. *The making of the Soviet system: essays in the social history of interwar Russia*. London: Methuen, 1985.

---. *Russia-USSR-Russia: the drive and drift of a superstate*. New York: New Press, 1995.

Löwy, Michaël, ed. *Marxism in Latin America from 1909 to the present: an anthology*. Translated by Michael Pearlman. Atlantic Highlands, N.J.: Humanities Press, 1992.

Marie, Jean-Jacques. *Le trotskysme*. Paris: Flammarion, 1970.

---. *Staline*. Paris: Fayard, 2001.

Mandel, Ernest. *La Longue marche de la révolution*. Paris: Galilée, 1975.

---. *Trotsky: a study in the dynamic of his thought*. London: NLB, 1979.

Mendel-Sztokfisz, Hersh. *Memoirs of a Jewish revolutionary*. London: Pluto Press, 1989.

Moreau, François. *Combats et débats de la IVe Internationale*. Hull, Québec: Éditions Vents d'Ouest, 1993.

Minguet, Simonne. *Mes années Caudron: Caudron-Renault, une usine autogérée à la Libération, 1944-1948*. Paris: Éditions Syllepse, 1997.

Naville, Pierre. *Trotsky vivant*. Paris: Maurice Nadeau, 1988.

---. *Le nouveau Léviathan*. 7 vols. Paris: Anthropos, 1957-1982.

Orwell, George. *Homage to Catalonia*. London: Secker and Warburg, 1938.

Pagès, Pelai. *El movimiento trotskista en España (1930-1935): la izquierda comunista de España y las disidencias comunistas durante la Segunda República*. Barcelona: Ediciones Península, 1977.

Pattieu, Sylvain. *Les camarades des frères: trotskistes et libertaires dans la guerre d'Algérie*. Paris: Syllepse, 2002.

Pereyra, Daniel. *Del Moncada a Chiapas: historia de la lucha armada en América Latina*. La Rioja: Editorial Canguro, 2000.

Plenel, Edwy. *Secrets de jeunesse*. Paris: Stock, 2001.

Prager, Rodolphe, comp. *Les Congrès de la Quatrième Internationale, 1930-1952*. 4 vols. Paris: La Brèche, 1978-1989.

Regler, Gustav. *The owl of Minerva: the autobiography of Gustav Regler*. Translated by Norman Denny. London: Hart-Davis, 1959.

Rousset, David. *La société éclatée: de la première à la seconde révolution mondiale*. Paris: Grasset, 1973.

Schwartz, Laurent. *A mathematician grappling with his century*. Translated by Leila Schneps. Boston: Birkhäuser, 2001.

Shachtman, Max, Hal Draper, C.L.R. James et al. *The Fate of the Russian Revolution – Lost Texts of Critical Marxism Vol. 1*. Edited by Sean Matgamna. London: Phoenix Press, 1998.

Sinclair, Louis. *Trotsky: a bibliography*. Aldershot: Scolar Press, 1989.

Serge, Victor. *Memoirs of a revolutionary*. Translated by Peter Sedgwick. London: Writers and Readers, 1984.

Solano, Wilebaldo. *El POUM en la historia: Andreu Nin y la revolución española*. Madrid: Libros de la Catarata, 1999.

Stinas, Agis. *Mémoires d'un révolutionnaire dans la Grèce du XXe siècle*. Paris: La Brèche, 1990.

Tennant, Gary. "The hidden pearl of the Caribbean: Trotskyism in Cuba." *Revolutionary History* Vol. 7, No. 3, Spring 2000.

Thirion, André. *Revolutionaries without Revolution*. Translated by Joachim Neugroschel. New York: Macmillan, 1975.

Tichelman, Fritjof. *Henk Sneevliet*. Paris: La Brèche, 1988.

Trotsky, Leon. *Writings of Leon Trotsky*. 14 vols. Edited by George Breitman, Naomi Allen, Sarah Lovell and Bev Scott. New York: Pathfinder Press, 1969-1979.

---. *My Life: an attempt at an autobiography*. Harmondsworth: Penguin Books, 1975.

---. *The Permanent Revolution and Results and Prospects*. Translated by John G. Wright and Brian Pearce. New York: Pathfinder Press, 1969.

---. *The Third International after Lenin*. Translated by John G. Wright. New York: Pioneer Publishers, 1957.

---. *Fascism: What it is and how to fight it*. New York: Pathfinder Press, 1996.

---. *The Revolution Betrayed: what is the Soviet Union and where is it going?* Translated by Max Eastman. New York: Merit Publishers, 1965.

---. *Le mouvement communiste en France*. Paris: Éditions de Minuit, 1967.

---. *The death agony of capitalism and the tasks of the Fourth International: The Transitional Program*. New York: Pathfinder Press, 1983.

---. *In defense of Marxism (against the petty-bourgeois opposition)*. New York: Pathfinder Press, 1970.

---. *Sur la deuxième guerre mondiale*. Edited and introduced by Daniel Guérin. Brussels: La Taupe, 1970.

---. *Stalin, an appraisal of the man and his influence*. Translated by Charles Malamuth. New York: Stein and Day, 1967.

Valtin, Jan. *Out of the night*. London: Fortress, 1988. (Also see Jean-François Vilar's engaging postcript to the French edition: *Sans patrie ni frontière*. Paris: Babel-Actes Sud, 1997.)

Van Heijenoort, Jan. *With Trotsky in exile: from Prinkipo to Coyoacan*. Cambridge: Harvard University Press, 1978.

Wald, Alan. *The New York intellectuals: the rise and decline of the anti-Stalinist left from the 1930s to the 1980s*. Chapel Hill: University of North Carolina Press, 1987.

Zeller, Fred. *Témoin du siècle*. Paris: Grasset, 2000.

Journals

Cahiers Léon Trotsky, journal of the Institut Léon Trotsky, Paris and Grenoble, 1979-2003.

Cahiers du CERMTRI, journal of the Centre d'études et de recherches sur les mouvements trotskystes internationaux, Paris, 1977- .

Dissidences, bulletin de liaison des études sur les mouvements révolutionnaires, <http://www.dissidences.net/>.

Quaderni del Centro Studi Pietro Tresso and *Quaderni Pietro Tresso*, journal of the Centro Studi Pietro Tresso, Foligno and Florence, 1986- .

Quatrième Internationale, French-language journal of the Fourth International. Brussels and Paris: 1944-1993.

La Vérité, newspaper of the French Committees for the Fourth International and the Internationalist Workers Party (POI), 1940-1944. Facsimile. Paris: EDI, 1978.

DANIEL BENSAÏD

Theses of resistance

The text below, written by Daniel Bensaïd for the journal "Viento Sur", represents a bold attempt to track the theoretical challenges faced by Marxism today. According to the author, the theoretical sterility of modern social democracy and other major political trends could result in Marxists sitting on their laurels and merely affirming orthodoxies inherited from the past. But, he insists, revolutionary theory must now attempt to come to grips with huge changes in the world since the collapse of Stalinism. His discussion ranges over modern imperialism, the balance sheet of the Soviet Union and similar countries, the class structure of contemporary capitalism, new nationalisms and community identities, social movements and political parties and postmodernist notions of difference and diversity - and much else besides. This is a dense and difficult text. We have made it available in English here because of its important insights into the weaknesses of and challenges to modern Marxism, and because of its significant signposts for future research and reflection; despite its difficulty, it will interest and provoke many of our readers.

"We are faced with a double responsibility: the transmission of a tradition threatened by conformism and the exploration of the uncertain contours of the future".

In the course of the last decade (since the disintegration of the Soviet Union and German unification), something came to an end. But what? Was it the "Short 20th Century" of which Eric Hobsbawm and other historians speak, beginning with World War I and ending with the fall of the Berlin Wall?

Or is it the short period that followed World War II, marked by the twin superpowers of the Cold War, and characterized in the imperialist centres by sustained capital accumulation and "Fordist" regulation?

Or again, is it the great cycle in the history of capitalism and the workers' movement, opened by the capitalist development of the 1880s, subsequent colonial expansion and the blossoming of the modern labour movement, symbolized by the formation of the Second International?

The great strategic analyses of the workers movement date to a large extent from this period of formation, before World War I: for example the analyses of imperialism (Hilferding, Bauer, Rosa

Luxemburg, Lenin, Parvus, Trotsky, Bukharin); the national question (Rosa Luxemburg again, Lenin, Bauer, Ber Borokov, Pannekoek, Strasser); party-trade union relations and parliamentarism (Rosa Luxemburg, Sorel, Jaurès, Nieuwenhuis, Lenin); strategy and the road to power (Bernstein, Kautsky, Rosa Luxemburg, Lenin, Trotsky).

These controversies constitute our history as much as those of the conflicting dynamics between revolution and counterrevolution inaugurated by the world war and the Russian Revolution.

Beyond the often intense differences over orientation and options, the workers' movement of that time displayed a relative unity and shared a common culture. What remains of this inheritance today?

In a very unclear editorial in the first issue of the relaunched "New Left Review", Perry Anderson estimated that the world has not been so lacking in alternatives to the dominant order since the Reformation. Charles-André Udry is more definite, arguing that one of the characteristics of the present situation is the "disappearance" of an independent international workers' movement.

We are then in the middle of an uncertain transition, where the old is dying without being abolished, and where the new is making an effort to emerge, caught between a past which has not been transcended and the increasingly urgent necessity of an autonomous research project, which would allow us to orientate ourselves to the new world opening before our eyes. Because of the weakening of the traditions of the old workers' movement there is a danger that, given the theoretical mediocrity of social democracy and other opponents to our right, we could resign ourselves to just defending old theoretical conquests, which today are of limited value. Certainly theory lives off debate and confrontation: we are always to a certain extent dependent on the debates with our adversaries. But this dependency is relative.

It is easy to say that the great political forces of what is called in France the "plural left", the Socialist Party, the Communist Party, the Greens, are not very stimulating in their approach to fundamental problems. But also it is necessary to remember that, in spite of their naiveté and sometimes their youthful excesses, the debates of the far left of the 1970s were much more productive and enriching than they are today.

We have then begun the dangerous transition from one epoch to another and we are in midstream. We must simultaneously transmit and defend our theoretical tradition, even if it is threatened by conformism, while at the same time boldly analysing these new times. At the risk of appearing shocking, I would like to face this test with a spirit I would describe as "open dogmatism". "Dogmatism", because, if that word gets a bad press (according to the media's common sense, it is always better to be open than closed, light than heavy, flexible than rigid), in all matters of theory, resistance to voguish ideas has its virtues. The challenge of versatile impressions and the effects of fashion demands that serious refutations are made before a paradigm is changed). "Open", because we should not religiously conserve a doctrinaire discourse, but rather enrich and transform a world view by testing it against new realities.

I would propose then five theses of resistance; their form deliberately emphasizes the necessary work of refusal.

- 1 Imperialism has not been dissolved in commodity globalization.
- 2 Communism has not been dissolved in the fall of Stalinism.
- 3 The class struggle cannot be reduced to the politics of community identities.
- 4 Conflictual differences are not dissolved in ambivalent diversity.
- 5 Politics cannot be dissolved into ethics or aesthetics.

I think these theses are demonstrable propositions. The explanatory notes explain some of their consequences.

THESIS 1: IMPERIALISM HAS NOT BEEN DISSOLVED IN COMMODITY GLOBALIZATION

Imperialism is the political form of the domination that corresponds to the combined and unequal development of capitalist accumulation. This modern imperialism has changed its appearance. It has not disappeared. In the course of recent centuries, it has undergone three great stages: a) that of colonial conquest and territorial occupation (the British and French colonial empires); b) that of the domination of financial capital or the "highest stage of capitalism" analyzed by Hilferding and Lenin (fusion of industrial and banking capital, export of capital, import of raw materials); c) after World War II, that of the domination of the world shared between several imperialist powers, formal independence of former colonies and dominated development. [1]

The sequence opened by the Russian Revolution has come to an end. A new phase of imperial globalization which resembles financial domination as it appeared before 1914, is what we have moved into. Imperial hegemony is now exerted in multiple ways: by financial and monetary domination (allowing control of credit mechanisms), by scientific and technical domination (a quasi-monopoly on patents), by the control of natural resources (energy supplies, control of trade routes, patenting of living organisms), by the exercise of cultural hegemony (reinforced by the huge power of the mass media) and, in the last instance, by the exercise of military supremacy (obvious in the Balkans and two Gulf Wars). [2]

Within this new configuration of globalized imperialism, the direct subordination of territories is secondary to the control of markets. From this results a very unequal and very badly combined development, new relations of sovereignty (disciplinary mechanisms like the debt, energy, food and health dependency, military pacts), and a new international division of labour.

Countries that seemed to be on the path of economic development until twenty or thirty years ago are again caught in the spiral of underdevelopment.

For example, Argentina is again mainly an exporter of raw materials (Soya has become its main export product). Egypt, which when ruled by Nasser's Arab nationalism in the 1950s boasted of its recovered sovereignty (symbolized by nationalisation of the Suez Canal), its successes in literacy (providing engineers and doctors for the countries of the Middle East) and the beginnings of industrialization (like Algeria under Boumedienne) is today becoming simply a paradise for tourist operators. After the two debt crises (1982 and 1994) and integration into NAFTA, Mexico appears, more than ever, as the dominated backyard of the "Northern colossus".

The metamorphosis of the relations of dependency and domination is reflected in particular through the geo-strategic and technological transformation of war.

During World War II, it was no longer possible to speak of war in the singular and of a single line of fronts, but of several wars overlapping with others. [3] From the end of the Cold War, the nature of the conflicts prevents any approach in terms treating the sides simply good and bad. All recent conflicts, with their unique combinations and multiple contradictions, show the impossibility of a simplistic response.

At the time of the Falklands War, opposition to the imperial expedition of Thatcher's Britain in no way forced Argentine revolutionaries to support the military dictators. In the conflict between Iran and Iraq, revolutionary defeatism in both countries was justified in face of two forms of despotism. In the Gulf War, international opposition to operation "Desert Storm" did not imply any support for the despotic regime of Saddam Hussein.

Globalization also has consequences in the structure of conflicts. We are no longer in the era of wars of liberation and relatively simple oppositions between dominator and dominated. From this results an intertwining of interests and a rapid reversibility of positions. It is an obvious reason to make a detailed balance sheet and to draw some lessons from the doubts, the errors (sometimes), and the difficulties that we could locate within the conflicts of recent years.

Reducing conflicts to an opposition between the simply "good" and the simply "bad" underlies much of the discourse of "human rights imperialism" which justified NATO's intervention in ex-Yugoslavia.

COROLLARY 1.1: INTERNATIONAL LAW AND THE DEMOCRATIC SOVEIGNTY OF NATIONS CANNOT BE DISSOLVED IN HUMANITARIAN ETHICS

Even though the function of the nation-state as it was constituted in the 19th century has undoubtedly been transformed and weakened, the era of interstate international law has nevertheless not arrived. Paradoxically, Europe has in the last 10 years seen more than 10 new formally sovereign states with more than 15,000 kilometres of new borders emerge. The vindication of the right to self-determination for the Bosnians, Kosovars or Chechnyans, is obviously, a vindication of sovereignty. It is this contradiction that is obscured by the pejorative notion of "sovereignism" under which nauseous nationalisms and chauvinisms are confused with legitimate democratic aspirations to a political sovereignty that offers resistance to the pure competition of all against all.

International law is still called upon to articulate two legitimacies: that, emergent, of the universal rights of human beings and citizens (of which certain institutions like the International Criminal Court constitute partial crystallizations); and that of interstate relations (whose principle goes back to the Kantian discourse about "perpetual peace"), on which institutions such as the United Nations rest. Without attributing to the UN virtues that it does not have (and without forgetting the disastrous balance sheet of its performance in Bosnia, Somalia or Rwanda), it is necessary to state that one of the aims pursued by the powers involved in operation Allied Force was to modify the architecture of the new imperial order in favour of new pillars, namely NATO (whose mission was redefined and extended during its 50th anniversary summit in Washington) and the World Trade Organization.

Emerging from the relationship of forces that emerged after World War II, the UN must undoubtedly be reformed and democratized (antiparliamentarianism does not prevent us supporting democratic reforms of the mode of scrutiny like proportionality and feminization), to the benefit of the General Assembly and against the closed club of the Permanent Security Council. Not in order to confer on it an international legislative legitimacy, but to ensure that a certainly imperfect representation of the "international community" reflects the diversity of interests and viewpoints. In the same way, we urgently need to develop a reflection around the European political institutions and the international judicial institutions like the Hague Tribunal, the emergency criminal tribunals and the future International Criminal Court.

EXPLANATORY NOTE 1: To update the notion of imperialism, not only from the point of view of the relations of economic domination (obvious), but as global system of domination (technological, ecological, military, geo-strategic, institutional) is of capital importance, precisely when seemingly intelligent people consider that this category became obsolete with the collapse of its bureaucratic foe in the East, and that the world is now organized around an opposition between democracies without adjectives (putting it another way, Western) and barbarism.

Mary Kaldor, who was, in the early 1980s, together with EP Thompson, one of the leaders of the campaign for nuclear disarmament against "exterminism" and the deployment of Pershing and Cruise missiles in Europe, now says that "the characteristic distinction of the Westphalian era between internal peace and foreign war, ordered domestic law and international anarchy, ended with the Cold War." We have now entered, it is argued, an era of "regular progress towards a global legal regime". It is what some call, without fear of the contradiction in terms, an "ethical imperialism", what Mary Kaldor calls "a benign imperialism".

THESES 2: COMMUNISM WAS NOT DISSOLVED IN THE FALL OF STALINISM

The ideology of neoliberal counter-reform, as well as trying to dissolve imperialism into the loyal competition of commodity globalization, tries to dissolve Communism into Stalinism.

Bureaucratic despotism would then be the simple logical development of revolutionary adventure, and Stalin the legitimate son of Lenin or Marx. According to this genealogy of the concept, the idea leads to the world. The historical development and the dark disaster of Stalinism are potentially there already in the notions of the "dictatorship of the proletariat" or the "vanguard party".

In reality, of course, a social theory is never more than a critical interpretation of an epoch. If we should seek gaps and weaknesses that make it lose its force in the face of the evidence and of history, that theory cannot be judged according to the criteria of another epoch. In this way, the contradictions of democracy, inherited from the French Revolution, a confusion of people, party and state, the decreed fusion of the social and the political, blindness in the face of the bureaucratic danger (underestimated in relation to the main danger of capitalist restoration), were propitious to the bureaucratic counterrevolution in 1930s Russia.

There are in the Russian Thermidorian process elements of continuity and discontinuity. The difficulty in accurately dating the triumph of the bureaucratic reaction relates to the asymmetry between revolution and counterrevolution. The counterrevolution is indeed not the reverse fact or the inverted image of the revolution, a sort of revolution in reverse. As Joseph de Maistre put it very well with regard to the Thermidor of the French Revolution, the counter-revolution is not a revolution in the opposite sense, but the opposite of a revolution. It depends on its own timescales, where ruptures are accumulated and complement each other.

If Trotsky dated the beginning of the Thermidorian reaction to the death of Lenin, he says that the counter-revolution was not completed until the beginning of the 1930s, with the victory of Nazism in Germany, the Moscow trials, the great purges and the terrible year of 1937. In her analysis "The Origins of Totalitarianism", Hannah Arendt establishes an apparent chronology that dates the coming of bureaucratic totalitarianism proper to 1933 or 1934. In Russia, USSR, Russia, Moshe Lewin brings to light the quantitative explosion of the bureaucratic apparatus of the state from the end of the 1920s. In the 1930s, the repression against the popular movement changed in scale. It is not the simple prolongation of what was prefigured by the practices of the Cheka (the political police) or the political jails, but a qualitative leap in which the state bureaucracy destroyed and devoured the party that believed it was able to control it.

The discontinuity demonstrated by this bureaucratic counter-revolution is central from a triple point of view. In relation to the past: the intelligibility of history that is not a delirious story told by a crazy person, but the result of social phenomena, conflicts of interests of uncertain outcomes and decisive events. With respect to the present: the consequences of the Stalinist counter-revolution contaminated a whole epoch and perverted the international workers' movement for a long time. Many paradoxes and impasses of the present (beginning with the recurrent crises in the Balkans) are not understandable without a historical understanding of Stalinism.

Finally, with respect to the future: the consequences of this counter-revolution, where the bureaucratic danger is revealed in its unexpected dimension, will still weigh for a long time on the new generations. As Eric Hobsbawm writes, "one cannot understand the history of the short 20th century without the Russian Revolution and its direct and indirect effects".

COROLLARY 2.1: SOCIALIST DEMOCRACY CANNOT BE SUBSUMED IN DEMOCRATIC STATISM

To portray the Stalinist counter-revolution as a result of the original vices of "Leninism" (a notion forged by Zinoviev at the 5th Congress of the Communist International, after the death of Lenin, to legitimise the new orthodoxy of reasons of state) is not only historically erroneous, it is also dangerous for the future. It would be then sufficient to have understood and to have corrected the errors to prevent the "professional dangers of power" and to guarantee a transparent society.

If the mirage of abundance is renounced this is the necessary lesson of this disastrous experience that would excuse society from choices and arbitrations (if necessity is historical, the notion of abundance is strongly relative); if we abandon the hypothesis of an absolute democratic transparency, founded on the homogeneity of the people (or of the liberated proletariat) and the rapid abolition of the State; if, finally, we remove all consequences of the "discordance of time scales" (economic, ecological, legal choices, customs, mentalities, art identify different temporalities; the contradictions of gender and generation are not resolved in the same way and at the same rhythm as class contradictions), then we should conclude that the hypothesis of the weakening of the state and of law, as separated spheres, does not mean their decreed abolition, unless the result is to be the statization of society and not the socialization of power.

Thus bureaucracy is not the annoying consequence of a false idea, but a social phenomenon. It certainly had a particular form within primitive accumulation in Russia or China, but it has its roots in scarcity and the division of labour. It manifests itself in diverse forms and different degrees of a universal manner.

This terrible historical lesson must lead to the deepening of the programmatic consequences drawn from 1979 onwards with the document of the Fourth International, "Socialist Democracy and the Dictatorship of the Proletariat", that specifically talks about political pluralism as a principle, the independence and autonomy of the social movements with respect to the state and to the parties, the culture of law and the separation of powers. The notion of "dictatorship of the proletariat" evoked, within the political vocabulary of the 19th century, a legal institution: the temporary emergency powers designated to the Roman Senate in opposition to tyranny, which was then the name given to arbitrary power. [4] Nevertheless it is too loaded with initial ambiguities and associated with too many bitter historical experiences to be still used. This note can nevertheless give us the chance to reframe the question of majority democracy, the relation between the social and the political, the conditions for the weakening of domination to which the dictatorship of the proletariat seemed under the form "finally discovered" of the Paris Commune, to have given an answer.

EXPLANATORY NOTE 2.1: The idea that Stalinism represents a bureaucratic counter-revolution, and not a simple more or less irreversible evolution of the regime arising from October, is far from meeting a general consensus. The opposite is true: liberal reformers and repentant Stalinists agree in seeing Stalinist reaction as the legitimate extension of the Bolshevik revolution. It is in effect the conclusion at which the "renovators" coming out of the orthodox Communist tradition arrive when they persist in thinking of Stalinism mainly as a "theoretical deviation" and not as a formidable social reaction.

Louis Althusser, in his "Reply to John Lewis", characterised Stalinism as an "economistic deviation". Many other theorists put the emphasis on theoretical error or deviation. This suggests it would be sufficient to correct this error to avoid the danger of bureaucratism. [5] The method of the "theoretical deviation", in perpetuating the parenthesis in the political analysis of the bureaucratic counterrevolution, is committed to a search for the original theoretical sin and not only leads to a recurrent liquidation of "Leninism", but, to a great extent, of revolutionary Marxism or the inheritance of the Enlightenment: from blaming Lenin, we quickly pass to blaming Marx... or Rousseau! If, as Martelli writes, Stalinism is primarily the fruit of "ignorance", a greater theoretical lucidity would be sufficient to prevent the professional dangers of power. [6] It's excessively simple.

EXPLANATORY NOTE 2.2: The French publication of Eric Hobsbawm's "Age of Extremes" was welcomed by the left as a work displaying intellectual health, a retort to historiography in the manner of Furet and historical judicialization in the style of Stéphane Courtois. This well-merited reception nevertheless runs the risk of leaving unclarified the extremely problematic aspect of the work.

Hobsbawm certainly does not deny the responsibility of the Thermidorian gravediggers: but he diminishes it, as if what happened, had to happen, by virtue of the objective laws of history. He hardly glimpses what could have been different.

And thus Hobsbawm arrives at what he considers the paradox of this strange century: "the most lasting result of the October Revolution was to save its adversary in war as in peace, inciting it to reform itself. [7] As if it was a natural development of the revolution and not the result of formidable social and political conflicts, of which the Stalinist counterrevolution is not the least! This "objectivization" of history reaches the logical conclusion that, in 1920, "the Bolsheviks committed an error, that seen retrospectively, seems capital: the division of the international workers' movement" [between Communism and social democracy - ed]. [8]

If the circumstances in which the 21 Conditions for joining the Communist International were adopted and applied demand a critical examination, we can nevertheless better understand the division of the international workers' movement not as a result of ideological will or a doctrinaire error, but of the original shock of the revolution and to the watershed between those who assumed its defence (critical, like Rosa Luxemburg) and those who opposed it and were associated with the holy imperialist alliance.

If the inter-war period means for Hobsbawm an "ideological civil war on an international scale", he is not talking about the fundamental classes, capital and the social revolution, but: progress and reaction, anti-fascism and fascism. Consequently he talks of regrouping "an extraordinary spectrum of forces". Within this perspective there is little space for a critical balance sheet of the German revolution, the Chinese revolution of 1926/27, the Spanish civil war and the popular fronts.

Avoiding any social analysis of the Stalinist counter-revolution, Hobsbawm is content with stating that, starting from the 1920s, "when the dust of the battles settled, the old orthodox empire of the Tsars resurged intact, in its essentials, but under the authority of the

Bolsheviks." For him, on the contrary, it is only in 1956, with the crushing of the Hungarian revolution, that "the tradition of the social revolution exhausted itself" and that "the disintegration of the international movement that was faithful to it" constituted the "extinction of the worldwide revolution" like a .re that is extinguished alone. In short, "it is above all by organization that the Bolshevism of Lenin changed the world". With this funereal phrase a serious critique of bureaucracy is avoided; it is simply considered as transitory, an "inconvenience" of the planned economy founded on social property, as if this property was really social and as if the bureaucracy was a small and lamentable expense rather than a counter-revolutionary political danger!

Hobsbawm's work has more the perspective of a "historian's history", than that of a critical or strategic history capable of discovering the possible options in the great turning points of events.

In "Trotski Vivant", Pierre Naville strongly emphasizes the reach of this methodological slant: "The defenders of the accomplished fact, whoever they are, have a much shorter vision than political actors. Active and militant Marxism is predisposed to an optic which is often contrary to that of history."

What Trotsky called "prognosis", says Naville, is more comparable to prophetic anticipation than to prediction or forecast. The same historians who find the sense of the event natural when the revolutionary movement has the wind in its sails, look for disadvantages in it when things are complicated and it becomes necessary to know how to swim against the current. It is hard for them to conceive the political imperative of "outlining history in the wrong direction" (in Walter Benjamin's formula). Naville says that this gives history the possibility of unfolding its retrospective wisdom, enumerating and cataloguing the facts, the omissions, and the errors. But, lamentably, these historians abstain from indicating the correct route that would have allowed a moderate to lead a revolutionary victory, or, on the contrary, to indicate a reasonable and victorious revolutionary policy within a Thermidorian period.

EXPLANATORY NOTE 2.3: It would be useful to do something that our movement has neglected: to take a deeper discussion about the notion of totalitarianism in general (and its relations with the epoch of modern imperialism), and on bureaucratic totalitarianism in particular. Trotsky frequently used this term in his book Stalin, without giving precision to its theoretical status. The concept could be considered very useful in approaching simultaneously certain contemporary tendencies (pulverization of the classes in masses, ethnicization and tendencial deterioration of politics) analyzed by Hannah Arendt in her trilogy on the origins of totalitarianism, and the particular form that they could take in the case of the bureaucratic totalitarianism. This would also allow that a vulgar and over-flexible employment of this useful notion serves ideologically to legitimize the opposition between democracy (without qualification or adjectives, consequently bourgeois, actually existing) and totalitarianism as the only pertinent cause of our time.

EXPLANATORY NOTE 2.4: To insist on the notion of bureaucratic counterrevolution does not imply in any way closing off a more detailed debate on the balance sheet of the revolutions in the century. On the contrary, we need to reappropriate it from a renewed perspective thanks to a better critical reframing. [9]

The different attempts at theoretical elucidation (theory of state capitalism, from Mattick to Tony Cliff, the new exploiting class, Rizzi to Burnham or Castoriadis, or the degenerated workers' state from Trotsky to Mandel), while they could have important consequences in terms of practical direction, are all compatible, through corrections, with the diagnosis of a Stalinist counterrevolution.

If Catherine Samary now proposes the idea that the fight against the nomenclature in power demanded a new social revolution and not only a political revolution, this is however not a simple terminological modification. According to Trotsky's thesis, enriched by Mandel, the main contradiction of the transitional society was between the socialized form of the planned economy and the bourgeois norms of distribution at the origin of bureaucratic parasitism and privileges. The "political revolution" consisted then in bringing the political superstructure into conformity with the acquired social infrastructure. Antoine Artous says that this forgets who "in the post-capitalist societies (not only in those societies that would be better not to describe as "post", as if they came chronologically after capitalism, when, in fact, they are determined by the contradictions of world-wide capitalist accumulation), the state is an integral part in the sense that it plays a determining role in the structuring of the relations of production; and it is by this slant that, beyond the common wage form, the bureaucracy, social group of the state, can be situated inside the relations of exploitation with the direct producers".

The continuation of this debate would have to call attention to the theoretical confusion related to the characterization of political phenomena in directly sociological terms, to the detriment of the specificity of the field and the political categories. Many ambiguities attributed to the category of "workers' state" arise from this. It is probably also the case with the notion of "workers' party", which tends to relate the function of a political force to a game of oppositions and alliances, to a deep social "nature".

THESIS 3: THE CLASS STRUGGLE IS NOT DISSOLVED IN COMMUNITY IDENTITIES

For too long a time, so-called "orthodox" Marxism attributed to the proletariat a mission according to which its consciousness would eventually meet with its essence, thus becoming the redeemer of all humanity. The disappointments of the following day are, for many, proportional to the illusions of the day before: by not having transformed itself into an "everything", this proletariat is then reduced to nothing.

We should begin by remembering that Marx's conception of the class struggle does not have much to do with university sociology. If in practice he does not have a statistical approach to the question, this is not mainly because of the embryonic state of the discipline then (the First International Congress of Statistical Data was in 1854), but for a more fundamental theoretical reason: the class struggle is a conflict inherent to the relation of exploitation between capital and labour that governs capitalist accumulation and the result of the separation between producers and means of production. We do not thus see in Marx any reductive, normative or classificatory definition of classes, but a dynamic conception of their structural antagonism, at the level of production, circulation and reproduction of capital: classes are never defined only at the level of the production process (the face off between workers and employers in the enterprise), but determined by the reproduction of the whole when the struggle for wages, the division of labour, relations with the state apparatuses and the world market enter into play. (From this it is clear that the productive character of labour that appears notably in Volume 2 of "Capital", with respect to the circulation process, does not define the proletariat. In their central aspects, these questions were dealt with and discussed widely in the 1970s, in clear opposition to the theses defended both by the Communist Party in its treatise on State Monopoly Capitalism, and inversely by Poulantzas, Baudelot and Establer.) [10]

Marx speaks generally of proletarians. In general, in the 19th century, people spoke of the working classes in the plural. The terms in German, "Arbeiterklasse", and English, "working class", stayed general enough, whereas the term "classe ouvriere", current in French political vocabulary, entails a restrictive sociological connotation prone to ambiguity: it relates to the modern industrial proletariat, excluding employees in the services and commerce, although these undergo analogous conditions of exploitation, from the point of view of their relation to private ownership of the means of production, location in the division of labour or still more in terms of their status as wage-earners and the amount of their remuneration.

Perhaps the term "proletariat" is theoretically preferable to that of "working class". In the developed societies it represents indeed between two thirds and four fifths of the active population. The interesting question is not its predicted disappearance, but its social transformations and its political representation, taking it as understood that the strictly industrial proletariat, even though it has undergone an effective reduction in the course of the last 20 years (from 35% to 26% more or less of the active population), is still far from the extinction. [11]

The real situation of the proletariat is revealed from an international perspective. Then what Michel Cohén calls "the proletarianization of the world" becomes evident. Whereas in 1900, wage-earning workers were around 50 million of a global population of 1,000 million, nowadays they are around 2,000 out of 6,000 million.

The question is then of a theoretical, cultural and specifically political order rather than strictly sociological. The notion of classes is in itself the result of a process of formation (see the introduction to EP Thompson's "Making of the English Working Class"), of struggles and of organization, in the course of which the consciousness of a theoretical concept and a self-determination born out of struggle is constituted: the sentiment of belonging to a class is as much the result of a political process of formation as of a sociological determination. Does the weakening of this consciousness, then, mean the disappearance of classes and their struggles? Is this weakening conjunctural (linked to the ebbs and flows of the struggle) or structural (the result of new procedures of domination, not only social but also cultural and ideological, what Michel Surya calls "absolute capitalism"), with the discourse of post-modernity representing its ideological expression? In other words, if the effectiveness of the class struggle is widely verified in everyday life, do post-modern fragmentation and individualism allow us to conceive the renewal of shared collectivities? Given the generalization of commodity fetishism and consumerism, the frenzy for the ephemeral and immediate, can durable political and social projects appear again, beyond moments of intense fusion without future? One of the high-priority theoretical tasks has to be not only related then to the sociological transformations of the wage-earner, but to the transformations underway in the wage relation in terms of regime of accumulation, as much from the perspective of the organization of work as of the legal political regulations and what Frederic Jameson calls "the cultural logic of late capitalism".

The critique of ultra-liberalism, in reaction to the counter-reform of the Thatcher- Reagan years runs the risk of being mistaken in its goal if, obsessed by the image of a commodity jungle after unrestrained deregulation, it does not measure the reorganizations and the attempts at re-regulation taking place. The domination of capital, as Boltanski and Chiapello note, could not last under the naked form of an exploitation and oppression without legitimacy or justification (there is no lasting imposition without hegemony, said Gramsci).

EXPLANATORY NOTE 3.1: What is on the agenda then is the redefinition of a global structure, a territorial organization, legal relations, based on the present productive forces (new technologies), the general conditions of accumulation of capital and social reproduction. It is in this framework that we see crises of transformation of the traditional political forces, Christian democracy, the British Conservatives, the French right, and the questioning of the function that they fulfilled since the war within the framework of the national state; and it is also in that framework that the transformation takes place of the Social-Democratic parties, whose elites, through the privatization of the public sector and the fusion of the private elites with the state elite, are increasingly organically integrated with the ruling strata of the bourgeoisie.

Given the weakness of the traditional bourgeois formations in the midst of reconversion, social democratic parties are often called often to assume temporary responsibility for the modernization of capital, dragging into their orbit the post-Stalinist parties without a project and most of the Green parties who lack the doctrinal wherewithal to resist accelerated institutionalization.

What it is outlined then, whether in the manifesto for a third way from Blair-Schröder, the projects for a social Europe of minimums, debated at the European summit in Lisbon, or the manoeuvres of the French employer's association on the subject of "social refoundation", is not a liberalism without rules, but a new wage relation in a framework of a previously unheard-of form of liberal-corporatism and liberal-populism. It would be dangerously short sighted to think that the only possible form of populism in the future will be the kind of backward-looking sovereignism of people like Pasqua and Villiers in France.

The crusade for wage-earning shareholders, private pension funds (to the detriment of solidarity), and the "refeudalization" of the social link (denounced by Alain Supiot) through the legal primacy of the individual contract (often synonymous with personal subordination in strongly unequal societies) over the impersonal relation with the law; all this outlines a new capital-labour corporative association, in which a small coterie of winners exist to the detriment of the mass of victims of globalization. In certain situations, this tendency is perfectly compatible with convulsive forms of national-liberalism in the manner of Russia's Putin or Austria's right populist leader Jörg Haider.

On the other hand, it is inoperative and possibly deceptive, to deal with the Haider case by analogy with the fascist movements of the 1930s, instead of linking it to the contemporary and probably unprecedented forms of the rightist danger. If it is right to participate in the mobilizations against Haider (without forgetting, nevertheless, the complacency of some of his affluent detractors towards Berlusconi, Fini, Millon, Blanc and others) we should not forget that Haider is firstly also a product of thirteen years of coalition between conservatives and Social Democrats, the lack of democracy in the EU and austerity policies that allowed him to arrive where he is.

It is important to consider the singular forms that reactionary threats can assume in today's world, the role of regionalisms in European reconfiguration, and the marriages between nationalism and neoliberalism. In his way, Haider is not lacking in black humour when he says "Blair and I against the forces of conservatism". [12] Our two parties "want to escape the rigidities of the beneficent State without creating social injustice ". Both want "law and order". Both consider that "the market economy, on condition that it is made flexible, can create new opportunities for wage-earners and companies." The Labour Party as well as the FPÓ has then a non-dogmatic approach "to that world transformation in which we live", where "the old categories of left and right have become irrelevant": "Are Blair and Labour right to accept the Schengen agreements and strict legislation about immigration?" Haider asks. And he responds, "If Blair is not an extremist, then Haider isn't either".

We should add that the regional populist Haider is as much in favour of NATO as Blair, and even more partisan than he in relation to the Euro!

EXPLANATORY NOTE 3.2: The recent appearance of an unpublished text of Lukacs from 1926, in defence of "History and Class Consciousness", invalidates to a certain point the ultra-Hegelian interpretations of Lukacs according to which the Party is the form finally discovered of the absolute Spirit. [*13*] Attacked for "subjectivism" by Rudas and Déborine during the 5th Congress of the Communist International, that of Zinovievist Bolshevization, Lukacs rejects the argument of Rudas, according to which the proletariat is condemned to act according to its "being" and the task of the party is reduced "to anticipating that development". For Lukacs, the specific (political) role of the party arises from the fact that the formation of class consciousness constantly clashes with the phenomenon of fetishism and reification. As Slavo Zizek says in his epilogue, the party plays for him the role of middle term in the syllogism between history (the universal) and the proletariat (the particular), whereas for social democracy, the proletariat is the middle term between history and science (incarnated by the educating party) and in Stalinism, the party uses the sense of history to legitimize its domination over the proletariat.

THESIS 4: CONFLICTUAL DIFFERENCE IS NOT DISSOLVED IN AMBIVALENT DIVERSITY

As a reaction against a reductionist representation of social conflict to class conflict, now - according to postmodernism and similar theories - is the hour of plurality of spaces and contradictions. In their specific and irreducible singularity, each individual is an original combination of multiple properties. Most of the discourses of post-modernity, like certain tendencies in analytical Marxism, take this anti-dogmatic critique as far as the dissolution of class relations in the murky waters of methodological individualism. Not only class oppositions, but more generally conflictual differences, are diluted then in what Hegel had already called "a diversity without difference": a constellation of indifferent singularities.

Certainly what passes for a defence of difference often comes down to a permissive liberal tolerance that is the consumerist reverse of commodity homogenization. As opposed to these manoeuvres of difference and individualism without individuality, vindications of identity on the contrary tend to freeze and naturalize differences of race or gender. It is not the notion of difference that is problematic (it allows the construction of structuring oppositions), but its biological naturalization or its identitarian absolutization.

Thus, whereas difference is mediation in the construction of the universal, extreme dispersion resigns itself to this construction. When one renounces the universal, says Alain Badiou, what prevails is universal horror.

This dialectic of difference and universality is at the heart of the difficulties that we frequently encounter, as illustrated by the discussions and the lack of understanding about equality or the role of the homosexual movement. Unlike the queer movement that proclaims the abolition of differences in gender to the benefit of nonexclusive sexual practices, up to the point of rejecting all logically reductionist lasting collective affirmation, Jacques Bunker, in his "Adieu aux norms", outlines a dialectic of affirmed difference to constitute a relationship of force faced with oppression and its desired weakening in a horizon of concrete universality.

Queer discourse proclaims, on the contrary, the immediate elimination of difference. Its rhetoric of desire, in which the logic of social necessity is lost, advances a compulsive desire of consummation. The queer subject, living in the moment a succession of identities without history, is no longer the homosexual militant, but the changing individual, not specifically sexed or defined by race, but the simple broken mirror of his sensations and desires. It is not in the least surprising that this discourse has received a warm welcome from the US cultural industry, since the fluidity vindicated by the queer subject is perfectly adapted to the incessant flow of interchanges and fashions. At the same time, the transgression that represented a challenge to the norms and announced the conquest of new democratic rights is banalized as a constituent playful moment of consumerist subjectivity.

Parallel to this, certain currents oppose the social category of gender with the "more concrete, specific and corporal" category of sex. They claim to transcend the "feminism of gender" in favour of a "sexual pluralism". It is not surprising that such a movement implies a simultaneous rejection of Marxism and critical feminism. Marxist categories would have provided an effective tool for approaching questions of gender directly related to relations of class and the social division of labour, but to understand "sexual power" and found an economy of desire different from that of necessity, it would be necessary to invent an independent theory (inspired by "Foucaltian" bio-politics).

At the same time, the new commodity tolerance of capital towards the gay market leads to the attenuation of the idea of its organic hostility towards unproductive sexual orientations. This idea of an irreducible antagonism between the moral order of capital and homosexuality allowed one to believe in a spontaneous subversion of the social order by means of the simple affirmation of difference: it was sufficient that homosexuals proclaimed themselves as such to be against it. The critique of homophobic domination can then end in the challenge of self-affirmation and the sterile naturalization of identity. If, on the contrary, the characteristics of hetero and homosexuality are historical and social categories, their conflicting relation with the norm implies a dialectic of difference and its overcoming, demanded by Jacques Bunker.

This problematic, evidently fertile when it deals with relations of gender or linguistic and cultural communication, is not without consequences when it concerns the representation of class conflicts. Ulrich Beck sees in contemporary capitalism the paradox of a "capitalism without class". Lucien Séve says that, "if there is certainly a class at one pole of the construction, the amazing fact is that there is no class at the other". The proletariat has seemingly dissolved in the generalized alignment; we are now obliged "to fight a class battle not in the name of a class but that of humanity".

Either, in the Marxist tradition, this is a banal reminder that the struggle for the emancipation of the proletariat constitutes, under capitalism, the concrete mediation of the struggle for the universal emancipation of humanity. Or, we have a theoretical innovation heavy with strategic consequences, for the rest of the book by Lucien Séve: the question of social appropriation is no longer essential in his eyes (it is logical, consequently, that exploitation becomes secondary with respect to universal alienation); social transformation is reduced to "transformations [of "disalienation"], no longer sudden, but permanent and gradual "; the question of the state disappears in that of the conquest of powers (the title, formerly, of a book by Gilles Martinet), "the progressive formation of a hegemony leading sooner or later to power in conditions of majority consent", without decisive confrontations (from Germany to Portugal via Spain, Chile or Indonesia, this "majority consent" nevertheless has never been verified so far! We find the same tone in Roger Martelli, for whom "the essential is no longer to prepare the transfer of power from one group to another, but to begin to give to each individual the possibility of taking control of the individual and social conditions of their life". The very legitimate anti-totalitarian theme of individual liberation ends then in solitary pleasure in which social emancipation is diluted.

If there is certainly interaction between the forms of oppression and domination, and not a direct mechanical effect of one particular form (class domination) on the others, it remains to determine with more precision the power of these interactions at a given time and within a determined social relation. Are we merely dealing with a juxtaposition of spaces and contradictions that can give rise to conjunctural and variable coalitions of interests? In which case the only conceivable unification would come from a pure moral voluntarism. Or else, the universal logic of capital and commodity fetishism affects all spheres of social life, to the point of creating the conditions of a relative unification of struggles (without implying, nevertheless, to be so discordant to social times, the reduction of contradictions to a dominant contradiction)?

We do not oppose to post-modern restlessness a fetishized abstract totality, but argue that detotalization (or deconstruction) is indissociable from concrete totalization, that is not an a priori totality but a becoming of totality. This totalization in process happens through the articulation of experience, but the subjective unification of struggles would arise from an arbitrary will (in other words, an ethical voluntarism) if it did not rest on a tendencial unification of which capital, understood here under the perverse form of commodity globalization, is the impersonal agent.

THESIS 5: POLITICS DISSOLVES NEITHER IN ETHICS, NOR IN AESTHETICS

Hannah Arendt feared that politics would finally disappear completely from the world, not only through the totalitarian abolition of plurality, but also by the commodity dissolution that is its dark side. This fear is confirmed by the fact of having entered an era of depoliticization, where the public space is squeezed by the violent forces that accompany economic horror and by an abstract moralism. This weakening of politics and its attributes (project, will, collective action) impregnates the jargon of post modernity. Beyond the effects of the conjuncture, this tendency translates a crisis of the conditions of political action under the impact of temporal space compression. The modern cult of progress means a culture of time and becoming to the detriment of space, reduced to an accessory and a contingent role. As Foucault indicated, space becomes the equivalent of death, fixed, immovable, opposed to the richness and dialectical fecundity of living time. The diabolical rotations of capital and the planetary widening of its reproduction overturn the conditions of its valuation. It is this phenomenon that expresses the feeling, so intense for two decades, of reduction of the duration of the instant and disappearance of the place in space. If the aesthetization of politics is an inherent recurrent tendency to crises of democracy, the admiration for the local, the search for origins, the ornamental overload and the manoeuvres of authenticity undoubtedly reveal a distressed vertigo verifying the impotence of politics faced with conditions that have become uncertain.

That politics is, in a first approximation, conceived as the art of the shepherd or that of a weaver, implies a scale of space and time, in which the city (with its public place and the rhythm of elective mandates) is the form. Citizenship is spoken of much more than the city and the citizen becomes unavailable in the general disorder of scales and rhythms. Nevertheless, we live still "in a period where there are cities and where the problem of politics arises because we belong to this cosmic period during which the world is delivered to its luck". Politics remains as the profane art of duration and space, of drawing up and moving the lines of the possible in a world without Gods.

COROLLARY 5.1: HISTORY IS NOT DISSOLVED IN A PULVERIZED TIME WITHOUT TOMORROW

The post-modern rejection of the grand narrative does not imply only a legitimate critique of the illusions of progress associated with the despotism of instrumental reason. It also means a deconstruction of historicity and a cult of the immediate, the ephemeral, the discardable, where medium term projects no longer have space. In the conjugation of the misadjusted social times, political temporality is precisely that of the medium term, between the fugitive moment and the unattainable eternity. It now demands more a mobile scale of duration and decision.

COROLLARY 5.2: PLACE AND SITE ARE NOT DISSOLVED IN THE FRIGHTFUL SILENCE OF INFINITE SPACE

The misalignment of the geographic mobility of capital (money and commodity) with respect to the relative or very conditional mobility of labour appears as the present form of unequal development that allows transfer of surplus value in the epoch of absolute imperialism: the unequal development of temporalities complements and relegates that of spaces. Consequently a mobile scale of territories, the importance acquired by the control of flows, the outline of a world order supported by a mosaic of weak, auxiliary states subalterned to commodity sovereignty.

However, collective action is organized in space: the meeting, the assembly, the encounter, and the demonstration. Its power is exerted in places and the very name of the event is related to dates (October, July 14, July 26) and to places (the Commune, Petrograd, Turin, Barcelona, Hamburg...) as emphasized by Henri Lefebvre, only the class struggle has the capacity to produce spatial differences irreducible to the single economic logic.

COROLLARY 5.3: STRATEGIC OPPORTUNITY IS NOT DISSOLVED IN ECONOMIC NECESSITY

The political sense of the moment, the opportunity, the bifurcation opened to hope, constitutes a strategic sense; that of the possible, irreducible to necessity; not the sense of an arbitrary, abstract, voluntarist possible, of a possible where everything would be possible; but a possible determined by an authority, where the propitious moment emerges for the decision adjusted to a project, an objective to be attained. It is, at the end of the day, sensed from the conjuncture, the response adapted to a concrete situation.

COROLLARY 5.4: THE OBJECTIVE IS NOT DISSOLVED IN THE MOVEMENT, THE EVENT IN THE PROCESS

Post-modern jargon willingly conciliates the taste for the event without history, happening without past or future, and the taste for fluidity without crisis, continuity without rupture, movement without objective. In the post- Stalinist slang of resignation, the collapse of the future ends logically at degree zero of strategy: to live the moment without enjoying, without ties! The ideologists of the disappointing tomorrow are satisfied, consequently, with preaching a "Communism that is no more", conceived as a "gradual, permanent movement, always unfinished, that includes moments of clashes and ruptures". [14] Advocating " a new concept of revolution" "a revolutionary process without revolution, a revolutionary evolution", or still more "to go further on without delay", towards an extra temporal immediacy. [15] Affirming that "the revolution is no longer what it was since there is no longer a single moment where evolutions crystallize", "there is no longer a great leap, a great decline, nor decisive threshold.' [16]

Certainly, there is no longer a single revolutionary moment, a miraculous epiphany of history, but moments of decision and critical thresholds. But the dissolution of the rupture in the continuity is the logical counterpart of a representation of the power possible to obtain with individual disalienation: "the progressive formation of a hegemony that leads sooner or later to power within the conditions of majority consent", says Lucien Sève. That "sooner or later" that defines a politics outside time seems at least imprudent in the light of the century and its tests (Spain, Chile, Indonesia, Portugal). Above all it ignores the vicious circle of fetishism and commodification, the conditions of reproduction of domination.

COROLLARY 5.5: THE POLITICAL STRUGGLE IS NOT DISSOLVED IN THE LOGIC OF THE SOCIAL MOVEMENT

Between the social and political struggles there are neither Chinese walls nor watertight compartments. Politics arises and is invented inside the social, in the resistance to oppression, the statement of new rights that transform victims into active subjects. Nevertheless, the existence of a state as separate institution, simultaneously false incarnation of the general interest and guarantor of a public space irreducible to private appetite, structures a specific political field, a particular relationship of forces, a language of conflict, where social antagonisms are pronounced in a game of displacements and condensations, oppositions and alliances. Consequently, the class struggle is expressed there in a manner that is mediated under the form of the political struggle between parties.

Everything is political? Doubtless, but only to a certain extent and up to a certain point. In the "last instance", if you wish, and in diverse ways.

Between parties and social movements, more than a simple division of labour, there operates a dialectic, reciprocity, and complementariness. The subordination of the social movements to the parties would mean a statization of the social.

Inversely, politics in the service of the social would rapidly lead to lobbying, corporative, a summary of particular interests without general will. Since the dialectic of emancipation is not a long and tranquil river: popular aspirations and expectations are diverse and contradictory, often divided between the exigency of freedom and the demand for security. The specific function of politics consists indeed of articulating them and conjugating them.

EXPLANATORY NOTE 5.5: Commenting on the disappearance of distinctive authentic political choices and the fact that the confusion of class alternatives is translated, in the Anglo-Saxon countries, in the tendency to the elaboration of rainbow platforms, conceived as incoherent collages of slogans that seek to catch all and whose priorities are obtained from the opinion polls, Zygmunt Bauman examines the capacities of the social movements to contribute an answer to the crisis of politics.

He emphasizes the way in which social movements undergo the effects of post-modernity: a limited lifespan, weak continuity, temporary aggregates of individuals reunited by the contingency of a unique difficulty and dispersed again as soon as the problem is solved. It is not the fault of programmes and leaders, says Bauman: this inconsistency and intermittency rather reflects the neither cumulative nor integrative character of suffering and shortage in these dissonant times. Social movements have then a poor capacity to demand great transformations and to pose great questions. They are poor substitutes for their predecessors, mass political parties. This impotent fragmentation is the faithful reflection of the loss of sovereignty of the state, reduced to a police station in the midst of commodity laissez faire. [17]

Zizek sees in the dispersion of the new social movements the proliferation of new subjectivities on the background of resignation, a consequence of the defeats of the century. This return to states, estates and bodies would be the logical consequence of detotalization and obscuring of class consciousness. Rejection of politics responds to the political limitation of the social made by the "political philosophies" of the last decade. However, the same gesture that tries to draw the limit between politics and non-politics and, to remove certain areas (beginning with the economy) from politics is "the political gesture par excellence". [18]

For Laclau, emancipation will indefinitely be contaminated by power, so that its complete realization would mean the total extinction of freedom. The crisis of the left would be the result of a double end to the representations of the future, under the form of the bankruptcy of bureaucratic Communism and the bankruptcy of Keynesian reformism. If a possible renaissance implies the "reconstruction of a new social imagination", the formula remains very vague since Laclau does not face any radical alternative.

In the controversy that opposes them, Zizek insists, faced with the new domesticity of the centre left, in "keeping open the utopian space of global alternative, even if this space must be left empty while it waits for its content". In effect, the left must choose between resignation and the rejection of the liberal blackmail according to which any perspective of radical change would have to lead to a new totalitarian disaster.

Laclau does not give up on the perspective of unification. He sees, on the contrary, in the radical dispersion of the movements, that makes unthinkable their articulation, the same failure of post-modernity.

Leaderless, reticular, decentred movements, forced by defeat to be cornered in a subaltern internalization of the dominant discourse? But also redeployment of the social movement in the different scopes of social reproduction, multiplication of spaces of resistance, affirmation of its relative autonomy and its own temporality.

All this is not negative if it goes beyond simple fragmentation and thinks about articulation. If this is not done, there is no another outcome than dispersed lobbying (the very image of subaltern as effect of domination on the dominated cf. Kouvelakis) or authoritarian unification by means of the word of the master, or a scientific vanguard, that would reduce political universalization to scientific universalization (a new avatar of "scientific socialism") or an ethical vanguard that would reduce it to the universality of the categorical imperative.

Without, in either case, approaching the process of concrete universalization by means of the extension of the area of the struggle and its political unification. There is no another way out in this perspective but to go back to the universalising theme, capital itself, and the multiple effects of domination produced by commodity reification.

NOTES

[1] See Alex Callinicos, "Imperialism Today", in "Marxism and the New Imperialism", Bookmarks, London 1994.

[2] See Gilbert Achcar, "La Nouvelle guerre froide", PUF, collection Actuel Mane, Paris 1999

[3] See Ernest Mandel, "The Meaning of the Second World War", Verso, London 1986.

[4] See V, Garonne, "Les révolutionnaires du XI-Xe siècle", Free Champ, Paris.

[5] Lucien Séve, "Commencer par les fins", La Dispute, Paris l999.

[6] Roger Martelli, "Le communisme autrement", Syllepse, Paris 1998.

[7] Eric Hobsbawm, "The Age of Extremes", Penguin, 1994.

[8] Ibid, page 103.

[9] See the contributions of Catherine Samary, Michel Lequenne, Antoine Antous in "Critique communiste", number 157, winter 2000.

[10] Nicos Poulantzas, "Classes in Contemporary Capitalism", NLB, London 1975; Baudelot and Establet, "La Petite bourgeoisie en France", Maspero, Paris 1970. See also the collection of magazines "Critique de l'" économie politique", "Critique communiste", "Cahiers de la Taupe".

[11] Stéphane Beaud and Michel Pialoux, "Retour sur la condition ouvrière", Fayard, Paris 1999.

[12] "Daily Telegraph", February 22, 2000.

[13] Rediscovered recently in Hungary, the Lukacs text has been published in English under the title "Tailism and Dialectic", followed by an epilogue by Slavoj Zizek, Verso, London, 2000.

[14] Pierre Zarka, "Un communisme á usage immediate", Plón, Paris 1999.

[15] Lucien Séve, "Commencer par les fins", op. cit.

[16] Rober Martelli, "Le communisme autremement", op. cit.

[17] "Letter from Zigmunt Bauman to Dennis Smith", in Dennis Smith, "Zigmunt Bauman, Prophet of Post modernity", Polity Press, Cambridge 1999.

[18] Zizek, op. cit., page 95.

The Mole and the Locomotive

Translation of Daniel Bensaïd's introduction to his book: "Résistances. Essai de taupologie générale", Fayard, Paris 2001.

'Well said, old mole. Canst work I' th' earth so fast? A worthy pioneer.' (Shakespeare, Hamlet I:5).

Our old friend is short-sighted. He is a haemophiliac as well. Doubly infirm and doubly fragile. And yet, patiently, obstinately, from tunnel to passage, he cheerfully continues his mole's progress towards his next invasion.

The nineteenth century experienced history as an arrow pointing in the direction of progress. The Destiny of the ancients and divine Providence bowed down before the prosaic activity of a modern human species, which produced and reproduced the conditions of its own improbable existence.

This sharpened sense of historical development was born of a long, slow movement of secularisation. Heavenly miracles were lost among earthly contingencies. Rather than illuminated by the past, the future now offered justification for the present. Events no longer seemed miraculous. Where before they had been sacred, now they were profane.

The railway, the steamship, the telegraph all contributed to a feeling that history was speeding up and that distances were getting shorter, as if humanity had built up enough speed to break free. It was the era of revolutions.

There was the revolution in transport and travel: in scarcely a quarter of a century, between 1850 and 1875, the great railway companies, the Reuter's agency and the Cook agency all emerged. The rotary press multiplied circulation figures. From now on it would be possible to travel around the world in eighty days. That hero of modernity, the explorer, heralded the air-conditioned exoticism of the tour operators.

There was the revolution in materials: with the triumph of the railway came the reign of coal, of glass and of steel, of crystal palaces and metallic cathedrals. High-speed transport, architectural transformations, the engineering of public health, altered the face of the city and transformed its relation to the suburbs.

There was a revolution in knowledge: the theory of evolution and developments in geology changed the place of man in natural history. The first murmurings of ecology explored the subtle metabolic interaction between society and its environment. Thermodynamics opened up new perspectives in energy control. The blossoming of statistics furnished calculating reason with an instrument for quantification and measurement.

There was a revolution in production: the "age of capital" saw the furious circulation of investments and commodities, their accelerated turnover, the great universal exhibitions, mass production, and the beginnings of mass consumption with the opening of the first department stores.

It was also a time of frenzy on the stock exchange, of speculation in real estate, of fortunes quickly made and equally quickly lost, of scandals, of affairs, of crashing bankruptcies, the time of the Pereires, the Saccards, the Rothschilds and the Boucicauts. And it was the era of empires and colonial divisions, when armies carved up territories and continents.

There was a revolution in working practices and social relations: mechanised industry usurped the workshop. The modern proletariat of the factories and the cities took over from the artisan class of tailors, joiners, cobblers, weavers. From 1851 to 1873, this growth in capitalist globalisation gave birth to a new workers' movement, which gained notoriety in 1864 with the creation of the International Working Men's Association.

This prodigious quarter of a century also saw the industrialisation of the arms trade, foreshadowing the "slaughter industry" and total war. It was the era of the social crime, "which does not seem like murder, because there is no murderer to be seen, because the victim's death appears natural, but which is no less a murder." [1] Between Edgar Allan Poe and Arthur Conan Doyle, the appearance of detective fiction, the development of rational modes of enquiry, and the scientific refinement of detection methods sum up the mindset of this period with its urban "mysteries": the loot passes from one hand to another, and all trace of the guilty party is lost in the anonymity of the crowd.

The railway was the perfect symbol and emblem of this rush towards technology and profit. Launched into a conquest of the future along the tracks of progress, these revolutions appeared to be the roaring locomotives of history!

The last quarter of the twentieth century offers a number of analogies with the third quarter of the nineteenth century, albeit on a completely different scale. Telecommunications, satellites and the internet are the contemporary equivalents of the telegraph and the railway. New sources of energy, biotechnologies and transformations in working practices are revolutionising production in their turn. Industrial manufacturing techniques increasingly make consumption a mass phenomenon. The development of credit and of mass marketing lubricates the circulation of capital. The result is a new gold rush (in the field of computers), a fusion of the upper echelons of the state with the financial elites, and relentless speculation with all its attendant Mafia scandals and spectacular bankruptcies.

The new era of capitalist globalisation is seeing the commodification of the world and a generalised fetishism. The time has come for a seismic overturning of national and international boundaries, for new forces of imperial domination which are armed right up to the stars. Yet the dream of this twilight era has already ceased to be one of infinite progress and great historical promises. Condemned to go round in circles on the wheel of fortune, our social imagination withdraws from history and, from Kubrick to Spielberg, escapes into space. The weight of defeats and disasters reduces every event to a dusty powder of minor news items, of sound bites which are skipped over just as soon as they are received, of ephemeral fashions and of faddish anecdotes.

This world in decline, prey to the inconsolable desolation of a faithless religiosity, of a commercialised spirituality, of an individualism without individuality, prey to the standardisation of differences and to the formatting of opinions, no longer enjoys either "magnificent sunrises" or triumphant dawns. It's as if the catastrophes and disappointments of the past century have exhausted all sense of history and destroyed any experience of the event, leaving only the mirages of a pulverised present.

This eclipse of the future imperils tradition, which is now seized by the conformism of remembrance commemorations. The past, notes Paul Ricoeur in La Mémoire, l'histoire, l'oubli, is no longer recounted so as to set us a task, but rather so as to institute a "piety of memory," a devout remembrance and a conventional notion of right-thinking. [2] This fetishism of memory claims to steer away from collective amnesia an era condemned to the snapshots of an eternal present.

Detached from any creative perspective, critical recollection turns to tired-out ritual. It loses the "unfailing consciousness of everything which has not come to pass." [3] The postmodern labyrinth is thus unaware of "the dark crossroads" where "the dead return, bringing new announcements." History, which is no longer "pushed towards the status of legend," no longer appears to be "illuminated by an internal light," contained "in the wealth of witnesses who look forward to the Revolution and the Apocalypse." [4] It crumbles into a dust of images or into the scattered pieces of a puzzle which no longer fits together.

The train of progress has been derailed. In the saga of the railway, sinister cattle trucks have eclipsed the iron horse. Already for Walter Benjamin, revolution was no longer comparable to a race won by an invincible machine, but rather to an alarm signal, fired so as to interrupt its mad race towards catastrophe.

That said, just as the reed outlives the oak, so the mole prevails over the locomotive. Though he looks tired, our old friend is still digging away. The eclipse of the event has not put an end to the hidden work of resistance which discreetly, when everything seems asleep, prepares the way for new rebellions. Just as the Victorian era's "growth without development" gave rise to the First International, just as the muted social war exploded in the uprising of the Communards, so too are new contradictions brewing in the great transformations of the present time.

However limited they might seem, the marginal conspiracies and plots active at any given moment are also fermenting the great rages of days to come. They herald new outpourings. They are the place of that "hard-fought advance" Ernst Bloch speaks of, "a peregrination, a ramble, full of tragic disturbances, seething, blistered with fissures, explosions, isolated engagements." [5] It is a stubborn advance made up of irreconcilable resistances, well-directed ramblings along tunnels which seem to lead nowhere and yet which open up into daylight, into an astonishing, blinding light.

Thus the underground heresies of the Flagellants, the Dolcinians and other Beguines paved the way for the likes of Thomas Münzer (1490-1525) to appear with his "apocalyptic propaganda calling for action," before his execution sealed the lasting alliance between the reformed priest and the country squire. After the egalitarian revolt of the Levellers, the great fear of the propertied classes cemented the puritan holy alliance between the bourgeoisie and aristocracy of England. After the creative upheaval of the French Revolution came Thermidor's period of restoration. After the great hope of the October Revolution followed the time of bureaucratic reaction, with all its trials and purges, its falsifications and forgeries, its disconcerting lies.

This recurrence of Thermidor has always bolted the door of possibility whenever it has been opened just a fraction. However, its "dull peace with the world" has never quite made its way to the obstinate mole, who is forever born anew from his own failures. It took no more than thirty years for the flames of 1830 or 1848 to rekindle the embers kept glowing by various hidden groups. It took only a few years for Jacobin radicalism to resurface, laden with new concerns, with the Luddites, and then with the Chartist movement of the English working class. [6] Less than twenty years after the bloody suppression of the Commune and the exile of its survivors, the socialist movement was already being born again, as if a timeless message had spread from generation to generation down a long line of conspiratorial whispers.

Whether they be failed or betrayed, revolutions are not easily wiped from the memory of the oppressed. They are prolonged within latent forms of dissidence, spectral presences, invasive absences, in the molecular constitution of a plebeian public space, with its networks and passwords, its nocturnal assignations and its thundering explosions. "One might imagine," warned an astute observer after the collapse of Chartism, "that all is peaceful, that all is motionless; but it is when all is calm that the seed comes up, that republicans and socialists advance their ideas in people's minds." [7]

When resignation and melancholy follow the ecstasy of the event, as when love's excitement dulls under the force of habit, it becomes absolutely essential "not to adjust yourself to the moments of fatigue." We should never underestimate the power, not of that daily fatigue which leads to the sleep of the just, but of the great historical weariness at having spent too long "rubbing history against the grain." Such was the weariness of Moses when he stopped on the threshold of Canaan to "sleep the sleep of the earth." The weariness of Saint-Just, walled up in the silence of his last night alive. Or the weariness of Blanqui, flirting with madness in his dungeon at Taureau.

Such too was the heavy fatigue which fell, in August 1917, upon the shoulders of the young Peruvian publicist José Carlos Mariategui: "We wake up ill from monotony and ennui. And we experience the immense desolation of not hearing the echo of the least event that might liven up our minds and make our typewriters rattle. Languor slips into things and into souls. Nothing remains but yawning, despondency and weariness. We are living through a time of clandestine murmurings and furtive jokes." [8] A few months later, this avid chronicler of resurrectional events came to find them at first hand in the old world of Europe, then in the throes of war and revolutions.

In reactionary times, obstinate progress becomes "a long, slow movement, itself patient, of impatience," a slow, intractable impatience, stubbornly at odds with the order that then reigned in Berlin, and that was soon to swoop down upon Barcelona, Djakarta or Santiago: "Order reigns in Berlin, proclaim the triumphal bourgeois press, those officers of the victorious troops, in whose honour Berlin's petty bourgeoisie waves its handkerchiefs and shouts hurrah. Who here is not reminded of the hounds of order in Paris, and of the bourgeoisie's bacchanalian feast on the corpses of the Communards? 'Order reigns in Warsaw! Order reigns in Paris! Order reigns in Berlin!' So it is that the proclamations made by the guardians of order spread from one centre to another of the global historic struggle." [9]

Then there begins the time, not for a passing reduction of speed, but for "inevitable revolutionary slowness," for maturation and ripening, for an urgent patience, which is the opposite of fatigue and habit: the effort to persevere and continue without growing accustomed or getting used to things, without settling into habit or routine, by continually astonishing oneself, in pursuit of "this desirable unknown" [10] which always slips away.

"At what moment in time could truth return to life? And why should it return to life?," wondered Benjamin Fondane in the very heart of darkness. [11] When? Nobody knows. The only certainty is that truth remains "in the rift between the real and the legal."

For whom? There are no designated heirs, no natural descendents, just a legacy in search of authors, waiting for those who will be able to carry it further. This legacy is promised to those who, as E. P. Thompson puts it, will manage to save the vanquished from "the enormous condescension of posterity." For "heritage is not a possession, something valuable that you receive and then put in the bank." It is "an active, selective affirmation, which can sometimes be reanimated and reaffirmed, more often by illegitimate heirs than by legitimate ones."

The event is "always on the move," but "there must be some days of thunder and lightning" if the vicious circle of fetishism and domination is to be broken. The morning after a defeat can easily lead to an overwhelming feeling that things must forever begin again from scratch, or that everything is suspended in an "eternalised present." When the universe seems to repeat itself without end, to keep on marking time, nevertheless the "chapter of changes" remains open to hope. Even when we are on the point of believing that nothing more is possible, even when we despair of escaping from the relentless order of things, we never cease to set the possibility of what might be against the poverty of what actually is. For "nobody can easily accept the shame of no longer wanting to be free." [12]

After twenty years of liberal counter-reform and restoration, the market-based order now seems inescapable. The eternal present no longer appears to have any future, and absolute capitalism no longer any outside. We are confined to the prosaic management of a fatalistic order, reduced to an infinite fragmentation of identities and communities, condemned to renounce all programmes and plans. An insidious rhetoric of resignation is used left, right and centre to justify spectacular U-turns and shameful defections, regrets and repentances [13]

And yet! A radical critique of the existing order braces itself against the tide, inspired by new ways of thinking resistance and events. In the vicious spiral of defeats, those engaged in defensive resistance sometimes harbour doubts about the counter-attack which is so long in coming; the hope of a liberating event then falls away from everyday acts of resistance, retreats from the profane to the sacred, and ossifies in the expectation of an improbable miracle. When the present drifts without past or future, and when "the spirit withdraws from a given era, it leaves a collective frenzy and a spiritually charged madness in the world." [14]

When it loses the thread of earthly resistance against the order of things, the desire to change the world risks turning into an act of faith and the will of the heavens. Then comes the tedious procession of smooth-talking potion sellers and charlatans, fire-eaters and tooth-pullers, pickpockets and cut-throats, relic-sellers and fortune-tellers, New Age visionaries and half-believers.

This is what happened after 1848, when the quarante-huitards of *A Sentimental Education* turned to commerce or looked to their careers. This is what happened after 1905, when disappointed militants became "seekers after God." This is what happened after May 1968, when certain faint-hearted prophets took it into their heads to play at angels, having played too much at monsters. In such situations, religious revivals and kitsch mythology are supposed to fill the gap left by the disappointment of great hopes.

Against renunciation and its endless justifications, those involved in the politics of resistance and events never give up looking for the reasons behind each loss of reason. But the disjunction of a fidelity to events with no historical determination from a resistance with no horizon of expectation is doubly burdened with impotence.

In a sense, resistance can take on an infinite variety of forms, from a concrete critique of existing reality to an abstract utopia with no historical roots, from an active messianism to a contemplative expectation of a Messiah who never comes, from an ethical politics to a depoliticised ethics, from prophecies seeking to avert danger to predictions claiming to penetrate the secrets of the future.

As for events whose political conditions seem evasive and compromised, it is all too tempting to treat them as moments of pure contingency with no relation to necessity, or as the miraculous invasion of repressed possibilities.

Thermidorian times, as everyone knows, see a hardening of hearts and a weakening of stomachs. In such circumstances, many people find nothing to oppose to the assumption that everything is likely to turn out for the worst, other than their willingness to settle for the lesser of the evils on offer; when this happens, the "flabby fiends" [15] congratulate each other, share a wink and pat each other on the back. Then the outgoing Tartuffe, "the old Tartuffe, the classical Tartuffe, the clerical Tartuffe," takes the "second Tartuffe, the Tartuffe of the modern world, the second-hand Tartuffe, the humanitarian Tartuffe, at any rate the other Tartuffe" [16] by the hand. This alliance of "two Tartuffe cousins" can last for a very long time, with "the one carrying the other, one fighting the other, one supporting the other, one feeding the other."

The veneration of victors and victories goes hand in hand with compassion towards the victims, so long as the latter stick to their role as suffering victims, so long as they are not seduced by the idea of becoming actors in their own version of history.

However, even in the worst droughts and most arid places there is always a stream - perhaps barely a trickle - which heralds surprising resurgences. Again, we must always distinguish between the rebellious messianism which will not give in, and the humiliated millennialism which looks instead towards the great beyond. We must always distinguish between the vanquished and the broken, between "victorious defeats" and unalleviated collapse. We must avoid confusing the consolations of utopia with forms of resistance that perpetuate an "illegal tradition" and pass on a "secret conviction."

There are always new beginnings, moments of revival or renewal. In the dark times of change and transition, worldly and spiritual ambitions, reasons and passions, combine to form an explosive mixture. Attempts to safeguard the old are mixed up with the first stammerings of the new. Even in the most sombre moments, the tradition on the rise is never far behind the tradition in decline. There is never any end to the secret composition of the uninterrupted poem of "probable impossibilities."

This obstinate hope is not to be confused with the smug confidence of the believer, or with the "sad passion" driven out by Spinoza. On the contrary, it endures as the virtue of "surmounted despair." For "to be ready to place hope in whatever does not deceive," you must first have despaired of your own illusions. Disillusioned, disabused, hope then becomes "the essential and diametrical opposite of habit and softening." Such hope is obliged constantly to "break with habit," constantly to dismantle "the mechanisms of habit," and to launch new beginnings everywhere, "just as habit everywhere introduces endings and deaths." [17]

To break with habit is to retain the ability to astonish yourself. It is to allow yourself to be surprised.

These untimely invasions, during which the contingency of events cuts a path through insufficient yet necessary historical conditions, make a breach in the unchanging order of structures and of things.

Crisis? What crisis is there today? There is a historical crisis, a crisis in civilisation, a stretched and prolonged crisis which drags on and on. Our ill-fitting world is bursting at the seams. As H.G. Wells predicted, the rift between our culture and our inventions has not stopped growing, opening up at the very heart of technology and knowledge a disturbing gap between fragmented rationalities and a global irrationality, between political reason and technical madness.

Does this crisis contain the seeds of a new civilisation? It is just as pregnant with unseen barbarities. Which will prevail? Barbarity has taken the lead by a good few lengths. It is becoming more difficult than ever to separate destruction and construction, the death throes of the old and the birth pangs of the new, "for barbarity has never before had such powerful means at its disposal to exploit the disappointments and hopes of a humanity which has doubts about itself and about its future." [18] We fumble our way through this unsettled twilight, somewhere between dusk and dawn.

Is it a simple crisis of development? Or indeed, rather than a sort of discontent within civilisation, is it a sorrow that gives rise to "myths which make the earth shake with their enormous feet"? If a new civilisation is to prevail, the old one must not be entirely lost, abandoned or scorned. Not only must it be defended, but it must also be ceaselessly reinvented.

The stubborn old mole will survive the dashing locomotive. His furry, round form prevails over the metallic coldness of the machine, his diligent good nature over the rhythmic clanking of the wheels, his patient smile over the sniggering steel. He comes and goes, between tunnels and craters, between burrows and breakouts, between the darkness of the underground and the light of the sun, between politics and history. He makes his hole. He erodes and he undermines. He prepares the coming crisis.

The mole is a profane Messiah.

The Messiah is a mole, short-sighted and obstinate.

The crisis is a molehill which suddenly opens out.

* * * * *

"People turn to soothsayers when they no longer have prophets" (Chateaubriand).

François Furet concludes The Passing of an Illusion with a melancholy verdict. "The democratic individual, living at the end of the twentieth century, can only watch as the divinely sanctioned order of history trembles to the core." To a vague anticipation of danger is added "the scandal of a closed future," and "we find ourselves condemned to live in the world in which we live." [19] Capital seems to have become the permanent horizon for the rest of time.

There will no more afterwards, no more elsewhere.

Death of the event.

End of story.

End of history.

Unhappily ever after.

But in fact there is always conflict and contradiction, there is always discontent in the midst of civilisation and crisis in the midst of culture. There are always those refuse servitude and resist injustice.

From Seattle to Nice, from Millau to Porto Alegre, from Bangkok to Prague, from the organisation of the unemployed to the mobilisation of women, a strange geopolitics is taking shape, and we don't yet which events will follow in its wake.

The old mole burrows on.

Hegel draws our attention to that "silent and secret" revolution which always precedes the development of a new way of thinking. Through the unreasonable detours of history, the cunning claws of the mole dig their own path of Reason. The mole is in no rush. He has "no need to hurry." He needs "long periods of time," and he has "all the time he needs." [Note missing in text] If the mole takes a backward step, it's not in order to hibernate but to bore through another opening. His twistings and turnings allow him to find the place where he can break out. The mole never disappears, he only heads underground.

Negri and Hardt say that the metaphor of the mole is a figure of modernity, they say that he has been surpassed by postmodernity. "We've come to suspect that the old mole is dead": his digging gives way to the "infinite undulations of the snake" and other reptilian struggles. [20] But such a verdict smacks of that chronological illusion whereby postmodernity is supposed follow on after a modernity that has since been consigned to the museum of ancient history. For the mole is ambivalent. He is both modern and postmodern. He bustles discreetly about in his "subterranean rhizomes," only to burst thunderously forth from the craters he makes.

On the pretext of giving up on history's metanarratives, the philosophical discourse of postmodernity lends itself to mystics and mystagogues: when a society runs out of prophets it turns to soothsayers instead. This is the way it goes, in periods of reaction and restoration. After the massacres of June 1848 and the 18th Brumaire of the younger Napoleon, the socialist movement was likewise seized by "Christolatry." "Look at these offspring of Voltaire," wrote one former Communard, "these former scourges of the church, now huddled together around a table, hands clasped in pious union, waiting hour upon hour for it to rise up and lift one of its legs. Religion in all its forms is once again the order of the day, and has become so very 'distinguished.' France has gone mad!" [21]

Pierre Bourdieu was right to distinguish mystical affirmation or divination from the conditional, preventive and performative stance of prophecy. "Just as the priest is part and parcel of the ordinary order of things, so too is the prophet the man of crisis, of situations in which the established order crumbles and the future as a whole is thrown into question." [22]

The prophet is not a priest. Or a saint.

Still less a soothsayer.

To ward off disaster, it's not enough to resist for the sake of resistance, it's not enough to wager on the possibility of a redemptive event. We must seek both to understand the logic of history and to be ready for the surprise of the event. We must remain open to the contingency of the latter without losing the

thread of the former. Such is precisely the challenge of political action. For history doesn't proceed in a vacuum, and when things take a turn for the better this never happens in an empty stretch of time, but always "in time that is infinitely full, filled with struggles." [23]
And with events.
The mole prepares the way of their coming. With a measured impatience. With an urgent patience.
For the mole is a prophetic animal.

NOTES

[1] Friedrich Engels, The Condition of the Working Class in England (Moscow and London, Progress Publishers/Lawrence & Wishart: 1973) 121 (translation modified).

[2] Paul Ricoeur, La Mémoire, l'histoire, l'oubli (Paris: Seuil, 2000).

[3] Paul Ricoeur, La Mémoire, l'histoire, l'oubli (Paris: Seuil, 2000).

[4] Ibid.

[5] ibid.

[6] See Edward P. Thompson, The Making of the English Working Class [1963] (London: Victor Gollancz Ltd, 1980).

[7] Henry Mayhew, London Labour and the London Poor: A Cyclopaedia of the Condition and Earnings of Those That Will Work, Those That Cannot Work, and Those That Will Not Work, 4 vols. [1861-1862] (New York: A.M. Kelley, 1967).

[8] José Carlos Mariategui, in El Tiempo (Lima) 16 August 1917.

[9] Rosa Luxemburg, "Order reigns in Berlin" (written on 14 January 1919, several days before her murder by the Freikorps despatched by a social democrat Minister of the Interior).

[10] Dionys Mascolo, Le Communisme (Paris: Gallimard, 1953).

[11] Benjamin Fondane, L'Écrivain devant la révolution (Paris: Paris-Méditerranée, 1997).

[12] Jacques Derrida with Marc Guillaume and Jean-Pierre Vincent, Marx en jeu (Paris: Descartes et Cie, 1997).

[13] Michel Surya, Portrait de l'intellectuel en animal de compagnie (Tours: Farrago, 2000) 11; see also Surya, De l'argent (Paris: Payot, 2000) 122.

[14] Karl Mannheim, Ideology and Utopia: An Introduction to the Sociology of Knowledge [1936] (London: Routledge, 1960) 192-196, quoted in E. P. Thompson, The Making of the English Working Class 419.

[15] "les monstres mous"

[16] Charles Péguy, Clio (Paris: Gallimard, 1931) 99.

[17] Charles Péguy, Note conjointe (Paris: Gallimard, 1942) 123.

[18] Georges Bernanos, La Liberté pour quoi faire? [1953] (Paris: Gallimard, 1995).

[19] François Furet, The Passing of an Illusion. The Idea of Communism in the Twentieth Century, trans. Deborah Furet (Chicago: University of Chicago Press, 1999).

[20] Antonio Negri and Michael Hardt, Empire (Cambridge, Mass.: Harvard University Press, 2000) 57.

[21] Gustave Lefrançais, Souvenirs d'un révolutionnaire (Paris: La Tête de feuille, 1971) 191.

[22] Pierre Bourdieu, "Genèse et structure du champ religieux," Revue française de sociologie 12 (1971) 331.

[23] Hegel, Leçons sur l'histoire de la philosophie (Paris: Folio Essais, 1990).

Hegemony and United Front

We publish below the summary of a contribution presented by Daniel Bensaïd, in the framework of the "strategy cycle" at the summer university of the LCR which was held in Port Leucate from August 24-29, 2007 (references have been changed to English language versions where available).

During the 1970s, the notion of hegemony served as a theoretical pretext to the abandonment without serious discussion of the dictatorship of the proletariat by most of the "Euro-communist" parties. As noted then by Perry Anderson, it did not however eliminate, in Gramsci, the necessary revolutionary rupture and the transformation of the strategic defensive (or war of attrition) into the strategic offensive (or war of movement) [1]

At the origins of the question

It appears from the reflections of Marx on the revolutions of 1848. Ledru-Rollin and Raspail were for him the representatives respectively of the democratic petty bourgeoisie and the revolutionary proletariat" Faced with the bourgeois coalition, the revolutionary parties of the petty bourgeoisie and the peasantry should ally themselves with the "revolutionary proletariat" to form a hegemonic bloc: "When he is disappointed in the Napoleonic Restoration the French peasant will part with his belief in his small holding, the entire state edifice erected on this small holding will fall to the ground and the proletarian revolution will obtain that chorus without which its solo song becomes the swan song in all peasant countries" [2]. This opposition of the victorious "choir" to the funereal "swan song" returns in 1871. The Commune is then defined as the "veritable representation of all the healthy elements of French society" and the "communal revolution" represents "all the classes of society which do not live from the labour of others".

From the end of the 19th century, the Russian revolutionaries used the term hegemony to characterise the leading role of the proletariat in a worker and peasant alliance against the autocracy and in the conduct of the bourgeois democratic revolution. From 1898, Parvus thus envisaged the necessity for the proletariat "to establish moral hegemony", and not only a majority power over the heterogeneous urban populations. That is why, according to Lenin, the social democrats "should go to all classes of the population", because the consciousness of the working class would not be really political "if the workers are not used to reacting against any abuse, any manifestation of arbitrariness, oppression and violence, whatever the classes which are the victims of it" Whoever draws the attention, the spirit of observation and the consciousness of the working class exclusively, or even principally, on itself is not a social-democrat, because, to understand itself, the working class must have a precise knowledge of the reciprocal relations of all the classes of contemporary society. This Lenin is much closer to the attitude of Jaurès to the Dreyfus affair, than that of a Guesde, advocate of a "pure socialism".

If the term hegemony does not appear in the controversy between Jaurès and Guesde on the implications of the Dreyfus Affair, its logic is nonetheless present in it [3] "There are times, states Jaurès, when it is in the interest of the proletariat to prevent too violent an intellectual and moral degradation of the bourgeoisie itself [...] And it is because, in this battle, the battle, the proletariat has fulfilled its task towards itself, towards civilisation and humanity, that it has become the tutor of bourgeois liberties that the bourgeoisie was incapable of defending". He was right, but Guesde was not wrong in his warning against the drifts and possible consequences of participation in a government dominated by the bourgeoisie.

For Jaurès, to the extent that the power of the party grew so did its responsibility. The time would come then "to sit in the governments of the bourgeoisie to control the mechanism of bourgeois society and to collaborate as much as possible in projects of reform" which are "the founding work of the revolution". Guesde, on the contrary, a socialist in a bourgeois government is never more than a hostage. The irony of history ensured that Guesde the intransigent ended his career as minister of a government of national and patriotic union, while Jaurès was killed as a probable obstacle to this Union.

Gramsci enlarges this question of the united front in fixing as its objective the conquest of political and cultural hegemony in the process of the construction of a modern nation: "The modern Prince must be and cannot but be the proclaimer and organiser of an intellectual and moral reform, which also means creating the terrain for a subsequent development of the national-popular collective will towards the realisation of a superior, total form of modern civilisation". [4] This approach is adopted within a perspective of passing from the war of movement characteristic of the revolutionary struggle in the "East" to a war of attrition (or of position), "alone possible" in the West: "This is what the concept of the united front seems to me to mean... Ilych, however, did not have time to expand his formula". [5]

This enlarged comprehension of the notion of hegemony allows us to specify the idea according to which a revolutionary situation is irreducible to the corporative confrontation between two antagonistic classes. What is at stake is the resolution of a generalised crisis of the reciprocal relations between all the components of society in a perspective which concerns the future of the nation as a whole. In fighting to make Iskra "a newspaper for all Russia", Lenin was not only already pleading in favour of an "effective collective organiser", he also opposed to the corporative localism of the committee men a revolutionary project on the scale of the whole country.

After the failure of the German revolution of 1923 and with the ebbing of the post war revolutionary wave, the task was not to proclaim the situation constantly revolutionary and advocate permanent offensive, but to undertake a prolonged struggle for hegemony through the conquest of the majority of the exploited and oppressed classes of the European workers' movement which was profoundly and durably divided, politically and in trade union terms. The tactic of the "workers' united front" seeking to mobilise in unity responded to this objective.

The programmatic discussion on a body of "transitional demands" starting from everyday concerns to pose the question of political power was the corollary of this. This debate, which was the object of a polemical confrontation between Thalheimer and Bukharin during the 5th congress of the Communist International, was first relegated to a secondary level, then disappeared from the agenda, in the course of successive purges in the Soviet Union and the CI.

In opposing to the dictatorship of the proletariat a notion of "hegemony" reduced to a simple expansion of parliamentary democracy or a long march through the institutions, the Eurocommunists watered down the message of the Prison Notebooks. Enlarging the field of strategic thought, upstream and downstream of the revolutionary test of force, Gramsci articulated the dictatorship of the proletariat to the problematic of hegemony.

In "Western" societies, the seizure of power is inconceivable without a prior conquest of hegemony, that is to say without the affirmation of a dominant/leading role inside a new historic bloc capable of defending, not only the corporate interests of a particular class, but providing an overall response to an overall crisis of social relations.

The revolution is no longer only a social revolution, but also and indissociably an "intellectual and moral reform", destined to forge a collective will both national and popular [6]. This perspective demands that we examine anew the notion of "withering away of the state" since the revolutionary moment does not lead to its rapid extinction, but to the constitution of a political state and a new ethic, opposed to the old corporate state

The notion of hegemony involves then for Gramsci: the articulation of a historic bloc around a ruling class, and not the simple undifferentiated addition of categories of discontent. the formulation of a political project, capable of resolving a historic crisis of the nation and social relations as a whole. These are the two ideas which tend to disappear today from certain not very rigorous usages of the notion of hegemony.

Is hegemony soluble in the post-modern soup?

At the end of the 1970s, the confused recourse to the notion of hegemony claimed not only to respond to the contemporary conditions of revolutionary change, but also to fill the gaping vacuum left by the unexamined liquidation of the dictatorship of the proletariat [7]. Orthodox Marxism, of the state or party, then appeared to have run out of steam.

The question re-emerged in the 1990s in a different context. To open a breach in the horizon drawn by a triumphant neoliberalism, Ernesto Laclau and Chantal Mouffe bent its interpretation, conceiving it as a chain of actors without a strong link, or as a coalition of social subjects refusing to subordinate themselves to a contradiction deemed to be principal. The exclusive hegemony of a class inside a composition of alliances which is more or less tactical and variable will be henceforth replaced by "chains of equivalence".

The struggles against sexism, racism, discrimination and ecological damage must be articulated to those of the workers to found anew a left hegemonic project. The difficulty resides in the modalities of this articulation. Bourdieu responds to this with a "homology" postulated between different social fields.

But if one renounces any structuring of the fields as a whole by an impersonal logic – that of capital as it happens -, the articulation or the homology can only represent the decree of a vanguard or an ethical voluntarism. This is the heart of the controversy between Zizek and Laclau. The latter envisages a first strategy which would conserve the category of class, in trying to reconcile it with the multiplication of identities represented by the new social movements, and placing it in an enumerative chain (movements of race, gender, ethnicity and so on... "without forgetting the good old workers' movement"!

The Marxist concept of class is however hard to integrate into this enumerative chain, to the extent that, in resigning itself to becoming the simple link in a chain, the proletariat would lose its privileged role. An alternative strategy would seek to expand the notion of working class at the risk of dissolving it in the magma of a wage earning class without cleavages or of the people as a whole, making it thus lose in another way its strategic function.

The "new social movements" thus seriously test a definition of socialism based on the working class and the Revolution with a capital R. Slavoj Zizek responds that the proliferation of political subjectivities, which seems to relegate the class struggle to a secondary level role, is only the result of the class struggle in the concrete context of globalised capitalism :In other words, the class struggle is not soluble in the kaleidoscope of identity or community categories, and hegemony is not soluble in an inventory of equivalences in the style of Prévert.

Political metamorphoses of the social actors.

Reporting an interview in which Stalin justified to an American journalist the single party for a society where the limits between classes are supposedly being eroded, Trotsky states in The Revolution Betrayed: "It appears from this that classes are homogeneous; that the boundaries of classes are outlined sharply and once for all; that the consciousness of a class strictly corresponds to its place in society. The Marxist teaching of the class nature of the party is thus turned into a caricature. The dynamic of political consciousness is excluded from the historical process in the interests of administrative order.

In reality classes are heterogeneous; they are torn by inner antagonisms, and arrive at the solution of common problems no otherwise than through an inner struggle of tendencies, groups and parties. It is possible, with certain qualifications, to concede that "a party is part of a class." But since a class has many "parts" – some look forward and some back – one and the same class may create several parties. For the same reason one party may rest upon parts of different classes. An example of only one party corresponding to one class is not to be found in the whole course of political history – provided, of course, you do not take the police appearance for the reality". [8] Thus he took a new road. If the class is susceptible of a plurality of political representations, there is some interplay between the political and the social.

The theorists of the 2nd International had noted that economic fragmentation prevented the realisation of class unity and made its political recomposition necessary but they regretted that this recomposition was incapable of establishing the class character of the social actors. The concept of hegemony appears to deal with this vacuum. Breaking with the illusions of a mechanical progress and of a one way historic direction, it demands the taking into account of historic uncertainty. One can, says Gramsci, only specify the struggle and not its outcome .

The distance maintained between the social and the political allows on the contrary envisaging their articulation as a determined possibility. Trotsky thus accused his contradictors of remaining prisoners of rigid social categories, instead of appreciating live historic forces. He saw the division of politics into formal categories of sociology as a theoretical corpse.

In the absence of conceiving politics according to its own categories (despite strong intuitions on Bonapartism or totalitarianism), he contented himself however with invoking these enigmatic "live historic forces", and calling on them to the creativity of the living. For him, as for Lenin, there was then no other outcome than to consider the Russian Revolution as an anomaly, a revolution out of time, condemned to hold come what may, while awaiting a German and European revolution, which did not come.

In Leninist discourse, hegemony designated a political leadership inside an alliance of classes. But the political field remains conceived as a direct and unequivocal representation of presupposed social interests. Lenin was however a virtuoso of the conjuncture, of the right moment, of politics practiced as a strategic game of displacement and condensations, as the contradictions of the system can erupt under unforeseen forms (for example a student struggle or a democratic protest), where one did not expect it. Unlike the orthodox socialists who saw in the world war a simple detour, a regrettable parenthesis in the march to socialism along the swept roads to power, he was capable of thinking of the war as a paroxysmal crisis requiring a specific intervention.

That is why, in contrast to an orthodoxy postulating the natural fit between social base and political leadership, the Leninist hegemony supposes a conception of politics "potentially more democratic than anything in the tradition of the Second International". [9]

The founding distinction between the party and the working class opens indeed the perspective of a relative autonomy and a plurality of politics: if the party is no longer confused with the class, the latter can have a plurality of representations. In the debate of 1921 on the trade unions, Lenin was logically with those who felt the need to support an independence of the trade unions in relation to the state apparatuses. Even if all the consequences of it are not drawn, its problematic implies the recognition of a "plurality of antagonisms and points of rupture". The question of hegemony, practically present but set aside, could thus lead to an "authoritarian turn" and the substitution of the party for the class. The ambiguity of the concept of hegemony must indeed be settled, either in the sense of a democratic radicalisation or in that of an authoritarian practice.

In its democratic sense, it allows the linking together of a multiplicity of antagonisms. It is necessary then to admit that democratic tasks are nor reserved solely to the bourgeois stage of the revolutionary process. In the authoritarian sense of the concept of hegemony, the class nature of each demand is on the contrary fixed a priori (bourgeois, petty bourgeois, or proletarian) by the economic infrastructure. The function of hegemony is reduced then to an "opportunist" tactic of fluctuating and varying alliances in the light of circumstances. The theory of combined and uneven development would necessitate on the other hand "an incessant expansion of the hegemonic tasks" to the detriment of a "pure socialism".

Hegemony and social movements

The Gramscian conception of hegemony sets up the bases of a democratic political practice "compatible with a plurality of historic subjects". That is also implied by the formula of Walter Benjamin according to which it was no longer necessary to study the past as before, historically, but politically, with political categories. [10]. Politics is no longer a simple updating of historic laws or social determinations but a specific field of forces reciprocally determined. Gramscian hegemony assumes fully this political plurality. It is increasingly difficult today to presuppose a homogeneity of the working class. Kautsky and Lenin had already understood that the class did not have immediate consciousness itself, that its formation went through constitutive experiences and mediations.

For Kautsky, the decisive intervention of intellectuals bringing science to the proletariat "from the outside" represented the main mediation. For Lukacs, it resided in the party, incarnating the class in itself as opposed to the class for itself.

The introduction of the concept of hegemony modifies the vision of the relationship between the socialist project and the social forces liable to realise it. It necessitates the renunciation of the myth of a great Subject, emancipation. It also modifies the conception of the social movements, which are no longer "peripheral" movements subordinated to the "working class centrality", but entirely separate actors, whose specific role depends strictly on their place in a combination (or hegemonic articulation) of forces. It finally avoids ceding the simple incoherent fragmentation of the social or removing it by a theoretical coup, by envisaging Capital as system and structure, of which the whole conditions the parts.

Certainly, the classes are what the sociologists henceforth call "constructs", or again according to Bourdieu "probable classes". But on what rests the validity of their "construction"? Why "probable", rather than improbable? From whence comes this probability, if not from a certain obstinacy of the real in inserting itself in the discourse. To insist on the construction of categories by language helps resist essentialist representations in terms of race or ethnicity. Still an appropriate material is necessary to this construction, and without this it is hard to understand how the real and bloody struggle of the classes has been able to haunt politics for more than two centuries.

Laclau and Mouffe admit to taking their distance from Gramsci, for whom the hegemonic subjects are necessarily constituted on the basis of fundamental classes, which supposes that any social formation is structured around a single hegemonic centre. A plurality of actors, plurality of hegemonies? This fragmented hegemony is contradictory with the original strategic sense of the concept, as unit of domination and legitimacy, or "leading capacity". In a given social formation there would exist, according to them , several nodes of hegemony. By pure and simple inversion of the relationship between unity and plurality, singularity and universality, plurality is no longer that which it is necessary to explain, but the point of departure of any explanation.

Plurality of the social or society in fragments

After the era of simple oppositions (People/Ancien Régime, Bourgeois/Proletarians, friend/enemy), the front lines of political antagonism become more unstable in increasingly complex societies. Thus, class opposition no longer allows a division of the whole of the social body into two clearly defined camps. The "new social movements" would thus have in common the concern to distinguish themselves from the working class and to contest the new forms of subordination and commodification of social life.

The result is a multiplicity of autonomous demands and the creation of new identities with a strong cultural content, the demand for autonomy being identified with freedom. This new "democratic imagination" will be the bearer of a new egalitarianism, worrying in the eyes of neoconservatives. For Laclau and Mouffe, to renounce the myth of the unitary subject on the contrary renders possible the recognition of specific antagonisms. This renouncement allows the conception of a radical pluralism allowing the updating of new antagonisms, new rights, and a plurality of resistances:: For example, feminism or ecology exist under multiple forms, which depend on the manner in which the antagonism is discursively constructed. There is a feminism opposed to men as such, a feminism of difference which seeks to revalorise femininity, and a Marxist feminism for which capitalism remains the main enemy, indissolubly linked to patriarchy.

So there will bed a plurality of formulation of antagonisms based on the different aspects of the domination of women. Similarly, ecology can be anti-capitalist, anti-productivist, authoritarian or libertarian, socialist or reactionary, and so on. Hence the modes of articulation of an antagonism, far from being predetermined, result from a struggle for hegemony". Behind this tolerant pluralism there is the spectre of a polytheism of values out of the reach of any test of universality. The war of the gods is no longer very distant.

Instead of combining the antagonisms at work in the field of social relations, Laclau and Mouffe rest on a simple "democratic expansion", where the relations of ownership and exploitation would be no more than one image among others of the great social kaleidoscope. The "task of the left" would no longer be then to combat liberal democratic ideology, but to "deepen and enlarge a radical pluralist democracy". The different antagonisms exacerbated by the social and moral crisis are nonetheless related to the ills of the world, to the disorders of generalised commodification, to the deregulations of the law of value, which under the pretext of partial rationalisations, generate a growing irrationality. What is the great factor of convergence and the movements gathered in the social Forums or the anti-war movements, if it is not capital itself?

Laclau and Mouffe end up logically by criticising the very concept of revolution, which would imply necessarily in their eyes the concentration of power with a view to a rational reorganisation of society. The notion of revolution would be by its nature incompatible with plurality. Welcome plurality! Exit the revolution! What is it that allows then a choice between the different feminist discourses, or the many ecologist discourses? How do we render them "articulable"? And articulable to what? How do we avoid plurality collapsing into itself in a formless magma?

The project of radical democracy definitively limits itself, for Laclau and Mouffe, to celebrating the plurality of the social. They must therefore renounce a unique space for politics to the profit of a multiplicity of spaces and subjects How to avoid then that these spaces coexist without communicating and that these subjects cohabit in reciprocal indifference and the calculation of egotistical interest? Following a "logic of hegemony", in the articulation between anti-racism, anti-sexism, anti-capitalism, the different fronts are supposed to support and strengthen each other, to construct a hegemony. This logic would threaten however that the autonomous spaces would become eroded in a single and indivisible combat. A "logic of autonomy" (or of difference) would allow on the contrary each struggle to maintain its specificity, but is at the price of a new closure between different spaces which tend to separate off from each other. But without convergences between diverse social relations, absolute autonomy would no longer be a more than a corporatist juxtaposition of identity-based differences.

Taken in a strategic sense, the concept of hegemony is not reducible to an inventory or a one to one sum of equivalent social antagonisms. For Gramsci, it is a principle of rallying of forces around the class struggle. The articulation of contradictions around the class relation does not imply their hierarchical classification in principal and secondary contradictions, or the subordination of autonomous social movements (feminist, ecologist, cultural) to the proletarian centrality. Thus, the specific demands of the indigenous communities of Latin America are doubly legitimate.

Historically, they have been deprived of their lands, culturally oppressed, dispossessed from their language. Victims of the steamroller of commodity globalisation and of imposed cultural uniformity, they are today revolting against ecological waste, the pillage of their common property, for the defence of their traditions. The religious or ethnic resistances to the brutalities of globalisation present the same ambiguity as the romantic revolts of the 20th century, caught between a revolutionary critique of modernity, and a reactionary critique nostalgic for the old days. The balance between these two critiques is determined by their relationship to the inherent social contradictions to the antagonistic relations between capital and labour. That does not mean the subordination of different autonomous social movements to a workers' movement itself in permanent reconstruction, but the construction of convergences of which capital itself is the active principle, the great unifying subject.

The concept of hegemony is particularly useful today in envisaging the unity in plurality of social movements. It becomes problematic on the other hand when it amounts to defining the spaces and the forms of power that it is supposed to help to conquer.

NOTES

[1] Perry Anderson, "The Antinomies of Antonio Gramsci", New Left Review I/100, November/December 1976

[2] K. Marx, "The Eighteenth Brumaire of Louis Bonaparte", Foreign Languages Press, Peking, 1978, p. 134

[3] Le Monde, May 16, 2003

[4] Gramsci, The Modern Prince, http://www.marxists.org/archive/gramsci/prison_notebooks/modern_prince/ch01.htm.

[5] Gramsci, Prison Notebooks, http://www.marxists.org/archive/gramsci/prison_notebooks/reader/q07-16.htm

[6] The idea of an "intellectual and moral reform" is taken from Renan and Péguy, whose thought had found an echo in Italy through the intermediary of Sorel.

[7] 7. See Etienne Balibar, Sur la dictature du prolétariat, Paris, Maspero, 1976; Louis Althusser and Etienne Balibar, Ce qui ne peut plus durer dans le Parti communiste, Paris, Maspero; Ernest Mandel, Critique de l'eurocommunisme, op. cit., and Réponse à Louis Althusser et Jean Ellenstein, Paris, La Brèche, 1979

[8] 8. L. Trotsky, The Revolution Betrayed, http://www.marxists.org/archive/trotsky/1936/revbet/ch10.htm.

[9] 9.E. Laclau and C. Mouffe, Hegemony and socialist Strategy, Verso, London, 2001, p.55. See Daniel Bensaïd, "La politique comme art stratégique", in Un Monde à changer, Paris, Textuel, 2003.

[10] 10. See Benjamin, "Paris: Capital of the Nineteenth Century", New Left Review, I/48, March-April 1968

DANIEL BENSAÏD

Thirty years after: A critical introduction to the Marxism of Ernest Mandel

The first edition by the Fondation Léon Lesoil of this Introduction to Marxism [1] dates from 1974. The date is not without importance. After the "oil shock" of 1973, Ernest Mandel was undoubtedly one of the first to diagnose the exhaustion of the post war boom and predict the reversal of the long wave of growth which followed the Second World War [2].

The debates inside the European left and workers' movement nonetheless remained marked by the illusion of an unlimited progress guaranteed by a Keynesian compromise and a "Welfare State". This optimistic vision of historical development gave the parliamentary left and the trade union apparatuses the hope of socialism at a tortoise pace, respectful of existing institutions while awaiting the political majority to join the social majority, in countries where – as illustrated in May '68 by the greatest general strike in history – waged labour represented for the first time two thirds of the active population. Mandel's Introduction is not then a text out of its time.

If it is still valid today for its pedagogic qualities in the presentation of the genesis of capitalism, the functioning of the economy, cyclical crises, combined and unequal development and so on, it nonetheless has a polemical dimension, of which certain essential elements have been amply confirmed by the thirty years which have passed since its publication:

▶ The logic of capitalism does not tend to a progressive reduction of inequalities, indeed to their extinction. If these inequalities had seemed to decline in the post-war period, it is not because of the generosity of a compassionate capitalism, but a social relationship of forces emerging from the war and the resistance, the wave of colonial revolutions, and the great fear which the ruling classes had experienced during the 1930s and the Liberation. Since the beginning, in the 1980s, of neoliberal counter-reform, the United Nations Development Programme (UNDP) has recorded from year to year a growth of inequalities, not only between countries of the South and the North but also between the richest and the poorest even inside the developed countries, and between the sexes despite the conquests of women's struggles. Not only were "the social state" and the "mixed economy" not eternal, not only were they not the solution finally found to the contradictions and crises of capitalism, but nothing, contrary to reformist illusions, is definitively won for workers as long as the possessors hold ownership of the great means of production and the levers of power. Thatcher and Reagan would not be slow to demonstrate it. And George W. Bush confirms in his manner that the epoch remains that of wars and revolutions.

▸ Private ownership of the means of production, exchange, communication, far from being diluted by popular share ownership, is undergoing an unprecedented concentration, and it exerts the corresponding effective power, not only in the economic sphere, but in the political and media sphere. For anyone who has not renounced the urgent necessity of "changing the world" the radical transformation of property relations in the sense of social appropriation remains just as decisive as at the time of the Communist Manifesto. And it is still truer at a time of globalisation, where capital commodifies everything, where the privatisation of the world extends to education, heath, living organisms, knowledge and space.

▸ If the state is not longer solely a "band of armed men" or the "night watchman state", if it fulfils sophisticated and complex functions within social reproduction, an "ideological function" as Mandel stresses, it is not for all that one relation of power among others (domestic, cultural, symbolic). It remains very much the guarantor and lock of power relations, the "boa constrictor" which hugs society in its multiple rings. So it is still necessary to open the road to its withering away as a specialised apparatus separated from society. All the revolutions of the 20th century, both victories and defeats, have confirmed this major lesson of the Paris Commune.

In spite of this verified pertinence, Mandel's Introduction to Marxism is marked by certain silences. The 1970s saw a new planetary rise of the movements for women's emancipation. The Fourth International adopted an important programmatic document on the question at its 11th world congress in 1979. However, in Mandel's text gender relations occupy at best a marginal place. In the same way, whereas ecological concerns came to the forefront notably following the movements against nuclear power stations or the Three Mile Island disaster, they are practically absent from the first edition of this Introduction.

That can probably be explained — but not justified — by the humanist and Promethean optimism which then coexisted for Mandel with an undisputable lucidity on the ambivalence of technical progress and the threat of barbarism.

This incoherence —or this contradiction – is confirmed by the role that he attributes, when responding to the challenges of the transition to a socialist society, to what I call "the joker of abundance". : "An egalitarian society founded on abundance, there is the goal of socialism". This march to abundance implies a growth of productive forces and the productivity of labour allowing a massive reduction of working time. If that is true in general terms, again it is necessary, under pain of falling into blind productivism and ecological insouciance, to subject these productive forces themselves to a critical examination. Incidentally, the notion of abundance is highly problematic. The supposition of an absolute abundance and of a saturation of natural needs indeed appears as a loophole before the necessity of establishing priorities and choices in the allocation of limited resources: how to allocate to health, education, housing, transport, how to decide the localisation of these investments and so on? Is there a natural limit to needs in the area of health or education? Like abundance, the needs are historic and social, thus relative.

One can consider rightly that the logic of commodity consumption arouses and nourishes artificial needs, luxuries, unnecessary, which a socialist society could very well do without. But the step from this to preaching austerity and frugality to the poor is one that certain ideologues of zero growth do not hesitate to cross. Who can distinguish between true and false needs, the good and the bad? Certainly not a group of experts, but the democratic arbitration of associated producers and users.

Indeed the recourse to the joker of abundance allows the avoidance, or at least simplification, not only of the question of social priorities in an ecosystem subject to limits and thresholds, but also that of democratic institutions in a society in transition to socialism. It is certainly not about demanding a democratic utopia delivered with the preconceived plans of a perfect city, but rather stressing the decisive importance of democratic forms in a society where the withering away of the state is in no way synonymous with a withering way of politics in the simple "administration of things" (as has been suggested by a formula unhappily borrowed - by Engels notably – from Saint-Simon).

One cannot reproach Mandel for this under-estimation, to the extent that he was the main writer of the resolution "Socialist Democracy and the dictatorship of the proletariat", adopted in 1979 by the 11th world congress of the Fourth International. But the fact is that his insistence on the theme of abundance tends to relativise the role of politics to the profit of a technical management of distribution without limits: "employees should replace the remuneration of labour by free access to all the goods necessary to the satisfaction of the needs of the producers.

Only in a society which ensures to humanity such an abundance of goods can a new social consciousness be born". It is right that he held this question of "free access", not only to certain health or educational services, but to basic needs in foodstuff or clothing, particularly close to his heart. It follows from the decommodification of the world and a veritable revolution in consciousness, for the first time putting an end to the biblical curse obliging humanity to win its bread "by the sweat of its brow".

Thus Mandel insisted: "Such abundance of goods is in no way utopian, on condition that it is introduced gradually, and starting from a progressive rationalisation of human needs, emancipated from the constraints of competition, the hunt for private enrichment, and the manipulation by advertising intended to create a state of permanent dissatisfaction among individuals. Thus the progress in living standards has already created a situation of saturation of consumption in bread, potatoes, vegetables, some fruits, indeed milk, and fat and pork products among the poorest section of the population of the imperialist countries. A similar tendency can be seen among undergarments, shoes, basic furniture and so on. All these products could be progressively freely distributed, without the intervention of money, and without involving significant increases in collective expenditure".

This logic of free access as the condition for the partial withering away of monetary relations remains current. The accent put on the conditions of "saturation of consumption" for the least poor part of the population in the richest countries leaves however in the shadows the weight of planetary inequalities and the relation of production to demographic evolution. The notion of "progressive rationalisation of human needs", although pertinent to the critique of the mode of life induced by capitalist competition, should not be confused with that of abundance, unless it is an abundance relative to a given state of social development which does not dispense with criteria and priorities in the use and distribution of wealth. Politics, and thus "socialist democracy" and not "the administration of things", remains then necessary to the validation of needs and to the fashion of satisfying them.

The most dated part of the 1974 Introduction, which most badly withstands the test of time and the events of the last quarter of a century is undoubtedly that concerning Stalinism and its crisis. Mandel here takes up the essentials of the analysis of the Left Opposition and Trotsky on the bureaucratic counter-revolution in the USSR and on its reasons: "The reappearance of increased social inequality in the USSR of today can be basically explained by the poverty of Russia immediately after the revolution, by the insufficiency of the level of development of productive forces, by isolation and the defeat of the revolution in Europe during the period of 1918-1923". This approach had the merit of stressing the social and historic conditions of the bureaucratic gangrene, unlike the currently fashionable reactionary historiography, typified by among others the Black Book of Communism – for which great historic dramas are only the mechanical result of what had germinated in the fertile minds of Marx or Lenin, when not simply "the fault of Rousseau". Serious contemporary research backed up by the opening of the Soviet archives (that of Moshe Lewin notably) confirms to a large extent the method of Mandel and sheds light on the different stages of the bureaucratic reaction in the Soviet Union.

Mandel takes up the classic analysis of the bureaucracy in the tradition of the Left Opposition to Stalinism: the bureaucracy is not "a new dominant class"; it "plays no indispensable role in the process of production"; it is "a privileged layer which has usurped the exercise of the functions of management in the Soviet economy and state, and on the basis of this monopoly of power granted itself lavish advantages in the area of consumption". Although debatable (the definition of classes – in the broad and historic sense, or in the sense specific to modern societies – is not clearly established by Marx himself) the distinction between fundamental classes and bureaucratic caste strives to analyse the singularity of an unprecedented phenomenon. It avoids the simplification of characterising the Soviet Union or China as "countries of socialism" requiring an unconditional fidelity, or inversely identifying them simply as an eastern version of western imperialisms.

But Mandel goes further. The bureaucracy is only a "privileged social layer of the proletariat". As such, "it remains opposed to the reestablishment of capitalism in the USSR which would destroy the very foundations of its privileges". The Soviet Union remains then "as in the days following the October revolution a society in transition between capitalism and socialism; capitalism can be restore there, but at the price of a social counter-revolution; the power of the workers can be restored there, but at the price of a political revolution which breaks the monopoly of the exercise of power in the hands of the bureaucracy."

Yet, by the 1970s, too much water had flowed under the bridges of history, and too many crimes had been committed, to claim such a continuity between the Soviet society of Brezhnev and the "the days following the October revolution". As for the ruling bureaucracy, it would not be slow in demonstrating that it was not such a determined "adversary" to the restoration of capitalism.

Even taking into account the didactic intention, this passage from the Introduction does not stand up to the test of time. On the one hand, in reducing the bureaucracy to a functional excrescence of the proletariat, Mandel excludes the hypothesis of its transformation into a dominant class in its own right. The disintegration of the Soviet Union and the velvet revolutions in eastern Europe have shown on the contrary that a substantial fraction of the bureaucracy can, on the basis of a "primitive bureaucratic accumulation" ripen into a gangster bourgeoisie. On the other hand the not very dialectical conception of the bureaucracy as "parasitic excrescence of the proletariat" underpins a debatable alternative between social counter-revolution and political revolution.

The hypothesis of a restoration of capitalism as "social counter-revolution" evokes in effect a symmetry between the events of the October revolution and this counter-revolution. Indeed, and this is the interest of the analogic notion of Thermidor, a counter-revolution is not a revolution in the opposite direction (a revolution reversed), but the contrary of a revolution, not a symmetrical event to the revolutionary event, but a process. In this sense, the bureaucratic counter-revolution in the Soviet Union certainly began in the 1920s and the collapse of the Soviet Union is only the final episode.

If it is necessary, in the light of the last twenty years, to criticize Mandel's reading of the situation, that should not prevent us from recognising that it had its uses in providing an orientation in the tumults of the century. It should also be recognised that it led to errors of appreciation, notably on the meaning of perestroika under Gorbachev or that of the fall of the Berlin wall. Having identified in "the decline of the international revolution after 1923" and in the backwardness of the Soviet economy, "the two main pillars of the power of the bureaucracy", Mandel deduced from this logically that with the rise of the Soviet economy (symbolised by Sputnik) and the renewed rise of the world revolution (in the colonial countries, but also in Europe after May 68), the hour of the political revolution was going to sound in the USSR and in Eastern Europe.

The overestimation of the "socialist gains" supposed to facilitate a political revolution democratising already constituted social relations thus led him in his book Beyond Perestroika (1989) to overestimate the dynamic of the political revolution and to underestimate the forces of capitalist restoration. In the same way his understandable enthusiasm concerning the overthrow of the Berlin Wall led him to interpret the event as a return to the tradition of Rosa Luxemburg and the workers' councils, after a long interval of reaction, and to underestimate the restorationist logic inscribed in the relationship of international forces. This was not only a manifestation of optimism of the will on his part, but very much an error of judgement stemming in part from theoretical roots.

His vision rested on the conception, shared inside the Fourth International since its congress of 1963, of a convergence between the "three sectors of the world revolution": the democratic revolution in the colonial countries, the social revolution in the imperialist metropolises, the anti-bureaucratic political revolution in the post-capitalist countries. In the 1960s, this perspective was not lacking in factual indices: the shock wave of the Chinese revolution, the victory of the Cuban revolution and the liberation struggles in Algeria, Indochina, and the Portuguese colonies; the anti-bureaucratic uprising in Budapest in 1956, the Prague spring in 1968, anti-bureaucratic struggles in Poland; resumption of social struggles and big strike movements in France, Italy, and Britain in the 1960s; the breakdown of the Franco and Salazar dictatorships.

In the midst of the 1970s, with the halting in 1975 of the Portuguese revolution, the monarchical transition in Spain, the split between Vietnam and Cambodia, the turn towards austerity of the European lefts, the normalisation in Czechoslovakia then the Polish coup, the winds had begun to change, and the "three sectors", far from converging harmoniously, had begun to diverge. Centrifugal forces triumphed. The bureaucratic struggles in the East were not led in the name of the workers' councils or self-management ("give us back our factories!") as was still the case in 1980 during the Solidarnosc congress, but were informed by mirages of western consumer society. The unequal reflux of deep-seated social revolutions announced the counter wave of "velvet revolutions", Foucault perceiving one of the first importance during the Iranian revolution of 1979.

Starting from a famous formula of Trotsky in the Transitional Programme, according to which "the crisis of humanity" is reduced to the crisis of revolutionary leadership, Mandel often had recourse, in taking account of an unexpected turn of events, to the notion of delay. The objective conditions of the revolution will be nearly always ripe, indeed overripe. Lacking only is the "subjective factor", absent or at least considerably behind in relation to the right moment of history.

If the old ideas continue to dominate the workers movement, "it is due to the force of inertia of consciousness which still retards material reality". This idea of a delay attributable to "the force of inertia of consciousness" is strange. Certainly, the owl of Minerva is said to only take flight at dusk, but the difficulties of class consciousness stem much more from the effects of the alienation of labour and commodity fetishism than to a reassuring time lag, suggesting that consciousness will come late, but will necessarily come. At least if it does not come too late?

The notion of "delay", like that of "detour", also frequently used by Mandel, presupposes a debatable normative conception of historic development. It introduces moreover a problematic relation (not very dialectical, whatever Mandel says in the methodological part of his Introduction – chapters 16 and 17 on the materialist dialectic and historical materialism) between the "objective conditions " and the "subjective conditions" of revolutionary action. If the objective conditions are as promising as is claimed, how can we explain the fact that the subjective factor is so unreliable in most of its incarnations? Such a divorce between the two could lead to a paranoia of treason: if the subjective factor is not what it should be, it is not in relation to certain relative limits of the situation and of the effective relations of forces, but because it is incessantly betrayed from within.

The very real capitulations, indeed betrayals of the bureaucratic leaderships of the workers' movement have certainly cost humanity dear in the past century (and will cost it still more dearly), but making this the main or exclusive explanatory factor of the disillusionments and defeats of the 20th century would end almost inevitably in a conspiracy vision of history which Trotskyist organisations have not always escaped. Mandel is happily much more nuanced. Thus he enriches his notion of objective conditions, "independent of the level of consciousness of proletarians and revolutionaries", including in this "the social and material conditions" (the strength of the proletariat) and "the political conditions", namely the incapacity of the dominant classes to govern and the refusal of the dominated classes to let them govern. Thus revised, the "objective conditions" include a strong dose of subjectivity.

There remain only among the said subjective conditions the level of class-consciousness of the proletariat and the level of strength of "its revolutionary party". They tend thus to be reduced to the existence, strength, consciousness, the maturity of its vanguard, detached from the complex mediations of the class struggle and the institutions. It opens the road to an exacerbated voluntarism, which is to the revolutionary will that which individualism is to the liberated individuality.

The risk of reducing the problem of modern revolutions to the sole will of their vanguard is compensated in Mandel by a sociological confidence in the growing extension, homogeneity, and maturity of the proletariat as a whole. Even if he concedes that "the working class is not entirely homogeneous from the point of view of the social conditions of its existence", the tendency to homogeneity would easily triumph in his eyes. It is supposed to overcome quasi-spontaneously the internal divisions and the effects of competition on the labour market: "Contrary to a widespread legend, this proletarian mass, although highly stratified, is seeing its degree of' homogeneity broadly increase and not decrease. Between a manual worker, a bank employee, and a minor civil servant, the distance is less today that it was a half century or a century ago, as regards standard of living, and as regards the inclination to unionise and go on strike, and as regards potential access to anti-capitalist consciousness."

In raising such a passage, we should, here again, remember its social context and the political issues at stake. Faced with changes in the division and organisation of labour which accompanied the long wave of growth, the question was posed of whether this amounted to the formation of a new working class and an extension of the proletariat, or on the contrary to the massive appearance of a new petty bourgeoisie.

The class alliances and formation of a new historic bloc would raise then new strategic questions, as argued in certain texts of Poulantzas, Baudelot and Establet, where some Maoist currents tried to find a European equivalent to the "bloc of four classes" dear to Chairman Mao. Mandel argued that the situation of the employees in the so-called tertiary sector was converging with that of the working class, from the viewpoint of the form (wage earning) and the average amount of income, their subaltern place in the division of labour, and their exclusion from access to ownership. This material convergence was confirmed by a cultural convergence, and verified by the behaviour of the new wage earning layers in the struggles of May 68 in France or the hot autumn in Italy: the old blind antagonism between blue and white collar, between workshop and office, blurred before solidarity in common struggle against exploitation and alienation.

If Mandel's argument was justified sociologically and strategically (the main problem was the rallying of the workers themselves and not the search for a class alliance or a new kind of popular front in the face of "state monopoly capitalism"), it transformed into an irreversible historic tendency the specific situation created by post war industrial capitalism and its specific mode of regulation. He thus took up on his own account the sociological gamble of Marx, that the strategic difficulties of the social revolution would be resolved though the development of large scale industry and the growing concentration of the proletariat in big units of production, itself favourable to a rise of the trade union movement, a strengthening of solidarities, and a raising of political consciousness.

If this certainly appeared to be the tendency of the 1960s and the early 1970s, the response of capital came quickly with the neoliberal offensive. Far from being irreversible, the tendency to homogenisation was undermined by the policies of dispersal of work units, intensification of competition on the world labour market, individualisation of wages and labour time, privatisation of leisure and lifestyles, the methodical demolition of social solidarity and protection.

In other words, far from being a mechanical consequence of capitalist development, the rallying of the forces of resistance and subversion of the order established by capital is an incessant task recommenced in daily struggles, and whose results are never definitive.

As he stresses in his foreword, Mandel accorded a major importance to the methodological chapters on the materialist dialectic and on the theory of historical materialism. This type of general exposé has its pedagogic virtues. The famous Elementary principles of philosophy by Georges Politzer have thus contributed to initiate dozens or hundreds of militants who were not intellectuals by training into the fundamental theoretical questions. But for Mandel as for Politzer, pedagogical vulgarisation has its price.

It gives the presentation of a theory the air of a manual, a little doctrinaire, and tends to present abstract universal laws – "the dialectic as universal logic of movement and contradiction", writes Mandel – overhanging their specific fields of validity. Thus if it is correct in the abstract that to" deny causality is in the final analysis to deny the possibility of knowledge", such a general affirmation says nothing on the numerous questions raised by the very notion of causality and on the different modes of causality, irreducible to the sole mechanical causality inspired by classical physics. Thus again, to define the dialectic as "the logic of movement" and the forms of passage from one state to another, tends to make of it a formal logic, detached from content, a system of general laws governing the singularities at work in the real world.

This is of course a discussion which would go far beyond the limits of this critical introduction to Introduction to Marxism. It is not however superfluous to indicate that its stakes are far from being negligible. Mandel's chapter on the dialectic finishes with the idea that "the victory of the world socialist revolution, the advent of a classless society, will confirm in practice the validity o revolutionary Marxist theory". The formula is to say the least adventurous. If victory should confirm the validity of a theory, the accumulation of defeats should reciprocally invalidate it. But who wins historically? On what timescale? Who is the judge? By what criteria? the questions are connected and run into each other, which goes back in the last instance to the idea that it can be done from science and scientific truth, or the relationship between truth and efficacy [3]. Here is another – very – long story.

Mandel's book, the questions and criticisms that it can raise thirty years after its first publication, are revealing of a time and the relationship of a revolutionary with his times. Roland Barthes could write of Voltaire that he was "the last happy writer", to the extent that he could express the world vision of a rising bourgeoisie, still capable of believing in all good conscience in the future of an enlightened and liberated humanity. In the same way one could say of Ernest Mandel that he was one of the last happy revolutionaries. This formula could surprise or shock, when used of a militant who knew the tests of war and imprisonment, who was witness to the tragedies of the century of extremes, who had to fight all his life against the dominant currents.

He was nonetheless a happy revolutionary to the extent that, despite the defeats and the disillusionments, he kept intact the confidence of the pioneers of socialism in the future of humanity, and the optimism which was theirs, at the threshold of a twentieth century which announced the end of war and human exploitation. For Ernest, classical humanist and man of the Enlightenment, the disillusionments of the twentieth century were only a long detour, or an annoying delay, which did not undermine the logic of historic progress. This obstinate conviction underlay both his greatness and his weakness.

July 25 2007

NOTES

[1] Published first in English as From Class Society to Communism.

[2] Ernest Mandel, La Crise, Paris, Champs Flammarion, 1978

[3] The Mandel quote relates to a certain extent to the criterion of the scientific status of a theory upheld by Popper, that of falsifiability"; a theory can only be called scientific if it is capable of being refuted in practice. That is why Marx' s theories, like those of Freud, which survive the denial of their prognostications or their therapeutic setbacks, cannot claim to be scientific. The argument rests on a series of debatable presuppositions, concerning both the relationship between the social sciences and the exact sciences, and the different forms of causality.

DANIEL BENSAÏD

Stalinism and Bolshevism

The following essay by Daniel Bensaïd represents a critical re-evaluation of Trotsky's well-known pamphlet Stalinism and Bolshevism (1937) [1]. It was written for the magazine Erre, published by supporters of the Fourth International in Italy.

There is a current fashion for roots and biblical genealogies: Hegel begat Marx, who begat Lenin, who begat Stalin... Those who are the most erudite go back as far as St. Paul or Plato. Real history and its social tissue disappear in these self-generating concepts. So the upheavals in this world are "Rousseau's fault" or "Plato's fault". Thus, by established descent, the Stalinist dictatorship is the allegedly logical continuation and the legitimate heir of the October Revolution, its mechanical and ineluctable consequence.

Adapted to today's fashionable thinking by the "historians" of the Black Book of Communism [2] and by repentant Stalinists like Annie Kriegel or Francois Furet, the refrain is nothing new, presenting Stalinism as the natural and legitimate offspring of Bolshevism.

In 1937, when Trotsky wrote this text "all reactionaries, Stalin himself, the Mensheviks, the anarchists and certain left doctrinaires" claimed that it was the case. This linear and fatalist conception of history recognizes neither leaps nor breaks nor choices of which road to take. It is simply a new theodicy of the spirit: the germ of all future developments was already contained in the initial idea that governs the world. Thus, the identification, pure and simple, of Bolshevism, of October, and of the Soviet state replaces the historical process of the class struggle on an international scale by a simple "evolution of Bolshevism in a vacuum".

When Trotsky, exiled in Coyoacan, made this point, it was a time when darkness was falling. The predicted future war was already casting its shadow over an obscure present [3]. After the second Moscow Trial came the trial of Tukhachevsky and the generals. The Barcelona Commune had just been crushed by the Stalinists. The news of Andreu Nin's assassination had just been confirmed.

In April, the former organizer of the Red Army received the commission presided over by the philosopher John Dewey, to refute the lies of the Stalinist trials. He was now busy assembling the material for his dossier on "Stalin's Crimes". In his eyes, this battle was just as important as the days of insurrection or the civil war. What was involved was nothing less than preserving a memory that was threatened with being effaced by lies and falsifications, in the same way as people suddenly disappeared from official photographs [4].

After a year's work, the commission made public, at a press conference held in New York on September 14th, 1937, the results of its enquiry, presented in a 600-page volume. It described the Moscow trials as "falsifications" and declared Trotsky and Sedov (his son) "not guilty". On learning the news, Trotsky cried out "Two lines! But two lines that will weigh heavily in the library of humanity".

We can understand from this reaction the importance that he then attached to this battle for memory, because there was no guarantee that the falsifications would not impose themselves as historical truth. Since then, they have been more than unmasked. That is not the least of the posthumous victories of the victims of Stalin, of the purges, and of the Gulag.

The opposite of a revolution

But in 1937, no one could know where the tragic spiral was going to end, the spiral of those "great political defeats", which, wrote Trotsky, on the first page of his pamphlet "inevitably provoke a reconsideration of values" in two opposing directions: an enrichment in the light of experience or a regression towards old ideas on the pretext of inventing "new truths".

The victory of Nazism in Germany, the defeat of the Spanish Revolution, the rise of the bureaucratic reaction in the Soviet Union, demanded in the middle of the 1930s a critical examination of the theoretical and moral heritage. The unfolding of the "short 20th century", the collapse of the so-called socialist camp, the neoliberal counter-reform begun in the 1980s, today require us to examine our consciences even more thoroughly.

But this self-examination does not start from nothing. It can, very fortunately, draw strength from the controversies and the combats of yesterday. In reality, if symbolically the fall of the Berlin wall and the disintegration of the Soviet Union mark the end of the historical cycle opened by the Great War of 1914-18, and by the October Revolution, the defeat of the great hopes of emancipation doesn't date from 1989 or 1991. That was only the second death of a corpse. Because already, a long time before, an interminable Thermidor had devoured the revolution.

How long ago exactly? That's the whole question. A litigious and controversial question. Many sincere communist militants have obstinately denied the fact of a bureaucratic counterrevolution on the pretext that they didn't find an event with a capital 'e' which was the perfect symmetry of October, the clear reversal of the process of which it was the initial act, a strict return to what existed before.

That is in reality an illusory search. More perceptive, the reactionary ideologue Joseph de Maistre had understood following the French Revolution, that the counterrevolution is not "a revolution in the opposite direction", but the "opposite of a revolution", a reaction that is rampant, asymmetrical, advancing in stages, sometimes pausing.

It is in this sense that the analogy with Thermidor, used by oppositionists in the Soviet Union from the 1920s onwards, was perhaps more pertinent than they themselves had imagined: a reaction which is not a reversal of time, a return to the past, but the invention of unforeseen historical forms.

In 1937 Trotsky was convinced that this bureaucratic counterrevolution had triumphed. The disastrous policy of the Communist International faced with the rise of Nazism and in the Spanish Civil War were proof of this, and even more so was its incapacity to draw the lessons of these catastrophes, other than the zigzag between the line of sectarian division of the "third period" and the line of subordination to bourgeois institution and allies in the framework of the popular fronts.

In the Soviet Union itself, forced collectivization had provoked the great famines and the mass deportations of 1932-33. The Soviet law of 1st December 1934 had legalized the emergency procedures of the Great Terror and of the great purge of 1936-38, the number of whose victims is estimated at 690,000. With the crushing of the urban and rural popular movements, this bureaucratic terror liquidated what was left of the heritage of October, cutting deeply into the ranks of the party and the army.

Most of the leaders of the revolutionary period were deported or executed. More than half of the 1900 delegates to the Congress of Victors of 1934 were eliminated in the space of a few months. Of the 200 members of the Central Committee of the Ukrainian Communist Party, there were only three survivors. The arrests in the army struck more than 30,000 cadres out of the 178,000.

Parallel to this, the administrative apparatus required for the undertaking of imposing this repressive regime and for the running of a brutally nationalized economy, exploded. According to the archives analyzed by the historian Moshe Lewin, the number of administrative personnel went in the space of 10 years from 1,450,000 in 1928 to 7,500,000 in 1939, and the total number of white collar workers rose from 3,900,000 to 13,800,000. The bureaucracy thus became a real, crystallized social force with its own interests.

A Bureaucratic Thermidor

In the 1930s however, this analysis was not easy to accept for communist militants who saw in the Soviet Union the strongest rampart against the rise of Nazism and who were marked by the hard battles conducted in the period of the line of "class against class" or by the heroic exploits of the international brigades in Spain. Unlike Social Democracy, whose bureaucratic degeneration occurred in the form of parliamentary bourgeoisification, the bureaucratic degeneration of the Communist International was masked by the rhetoric of the "defence of the Soviet Union". This is the epoch that Isaac Deutscher pertinently defined as the time of "bureaucratised heroism" to which the accounts of Anna Larina Bukharina, of Victor Serge, of Jan Valtin, of Alexander Zimin and of so many others bear poignant witness.

However, each in their own way, authors as different as Walter Benjamin (in his conversations with Brecht) or Hannah Arendt (in the Origins of Totalitarianism) have discovered the same point of historical inflection. This judgement has been largely confirmed by more recent historical work, such as that of Moshe Lewin, Eric Hobsbawm, or Pierre Broué, taking advantage of the opening of the Soviet archives (see in particular The Soviet Century by Moshe Lewin, 2003). In the course of the decade of the 1930s, Soviet society underwent a thoroughgoing metamorphosis under the bureaucratic knout. No country in the world had previously experienced such a rapid transformation, carried out by the iron fist of an autocratic bureaucracy.

The recent memory of Brezhnevite stagnation or the senility of Chernenko leave the impression of an immobile conservatism, whereas the rising bureaucracy was on the contrary brutally dynamic and enterprising. From 1926-30to 1930 the cities grew by 30 million inhabitants. Their population went from 18% to 33% of the total population. Under the first five year plan, the rate of growth was 44%, as much as during the whole period from 1897 to 1926. he wage labour force rose from 10 to 22 million workers.

The result was a "massive ruralisation" of the cities, which became an enormous site for the spread of literacy and education, the imposition of work discipline by a forced march, the exaltation of nationalism and the rewarding of careerism, the crystallization of a new bureaucratic conformism. In this great hurly-burly, as Moshe Lewin ironically remarks, society had almost become the famous "classless society", not because class relations had withered away, but because all the classes were "shapeless and in fusion".

What was then taking place was not the personal rivalries which so enrapture our medias today, it was not the outcome of a "match between Stalin and Trotsky" but really "an antagonism between the bureaucracy and the proletariat", a confrontation "between two worlds, two programmmes, two moralities", expressed by strategically opposed positions on the Chinese Revolution, on how to fight fascism, on the orientation of the Soviet economy, on the Spanish Civil War, on the coming war.

Trotsky and the left oppositionists abundantly used the analogy with Thermidor to describe the process of bureaucratic counterrevolution. They wished in this way to underline that Thermidor was not a restoration, a return to the *ancien regime*, but a counterrevolution in the revolution: the empire that resulted thus appeared as a grey zone where revolutionary aspirations were still tangled up with the consolidation of a new order of class rule.

Chateaubriand's *Memoires d'Outre-tombe* perfectly illustrates the pertinence of the analogy. We clearly find in Stalin the characteristic traits of the Thermidorian parvenu, a sort of more mediocre Napoleon. Both of them rose on the receding revolutionary wave, on the suppression of the earlier aspirations for emancipation, even though they spread certain of the effects of these aspirations in spite of themselves: "That Bonaparte, continuing the successes of the Republic, sowed everywhere the principle of independence, that his victories helped loosen the links between peoples and kings, tore these peoples free from the power of old customs and old ideas: that in this sense he pursued social liberation, all that I can in no way contest: but that of his own will, he consciously worked for the political and civil liberation of nations; that he established the most narrow despotism with the idea of giving Europe, and France in particular, the broadest constitution; that he was only a tribune disguised as a tyrant, that is a supposition that it is impossible for me to adopt: the revolution, which was Napoleon's source, soon appeared to him as an enemy; he fought it ceaselessly" [5]. Like him, Stalin could have said: "I have conjured away the terrible spirit of novelty which was bestriding the world".

So Thermidor was not the restoration. But the restoration followed Thermidor, just as in Russia the liberal restoration succeeded the bureaucratic Thermidor. But the restoration, that sinister epoch where the names of Robespierre, Marat, Saint-Just, could not be pronounced, only lasted for a time.

The (Original) Sin of Statism?

In his pamphlet, Trotsky polemicised against the anarchist thesis according to which the evils of Stalinism came from a defect of statism that was part of the Marxist programme. It is however enough to (re-)read the criticism by Marx and Engels of the programmes of Gotha and Erfurt, or *State and Revolution*, written hastily by Lenin in the middle of the revolutionary torment, to see that the problem lies not in the theory, but in very concrete social contradictions.

Do we really need to remind people that Marx conducted a polemic on two fronts, against the illusions in the social struggle that led the anarchists to misunderstand the specificity of political struggle, but also against the statist socialism of Lassalle.

And although he opposed the abstract negation of the state and of all authority by Bakunin, it was in order to oppose this with the theme of the "withering away" or "extinction" of the state as a separate and fetishised body, insisting on the historical conditions of such a withering away. It was in reality not a question of proclaiming this, but of attaining the real conditions for it: a massive reduction of forced working time, the socialization of administrative functions, a radical transformation of the social division of labour and of the relations between town and country, etc.

All these things cannot be done in a day by waving a magic wand: taking power is an act, an event, a moment of decision and of truth; it is only the means and the beginning of a process of permanent revolution. The other aspect of the polemic with Bakunin, which is too often forgotten, concerned democracy: the rejection of all authority, including the authority of a majority decision, in the name of freedom of the individual or of active minorities, implies at the end of the day the rejection of any democratic constraint [6]

As for Lenin, State and Revolution is a text of a libertarian communist tone which puts the emphasis on the destruction of the old bureaucratic state machine and on all the emerging forms of self emancipation. Trotsky recalled that in this perspective, Lenin had envisaged leaving some territories for the anarchists to conduct their community experiments.

If there was a theoretical error, it lies rather in the libertarian excesses of this text and in its optimism concerning the rhythms of the predicted withering away of political and juridical institutions.

Certainly this vision was counting on the rapid extension of the revolution in Europe, but it omitted to think about the institutional and juridical forms necessary for the period of transition. Thus, the founding texts of the first four congresses of the Communist International or the 1921 trade union debate demonstrate an insufficient clarification of the relations between the state, the soviets, the parties and the unions.

While indicating his "full agreement" with the anarchists "in regard to the final goal of the liquidation of the state", Trotsky drew the lessons of this experience, further enriched by the experience of the Spanish Civil War and of the entry of the anarchists themselves into the government of Largo Caballero in the autumn of 1936: "The victory cannot be thought of as a single event: it must be considered in the perspective of a historic epoch". So that, if it is "absolutely undeniable" that "the domination of a single party served as the juridical point of departure for the totalitarian Stalinist system (...) the reason for this development" was not consubstantial with Bolshevism, and "to deduce Stalinism from Bolshevism is exactly the same thing as to deduce, in a larger sense, counterrevolution from revolution".

On the other hand, the conception of the party and its vanguard role was still problematic in 1937. Trotsky underlined then that "the prohibition of the other Soviet parties(...)did not flow from any 'theory' of Bolshevism", but was a measure of defence of a revolution which, although "signalling a tremendous danger" was imposed to defend the revolution in a situation of civil war.

However, the problem remains: the victory in this internal war against the Whites and their international allies led in 1921 to the New Economic Policy, aimed at getting an exhausted country back on its feet; it was not associated with a democratic opening on the political level, an opening that was all the more necessary because "the culture of war" was the crucible of a bureaucratic brutality which the national question, among others, revealed to Lenin in the last months of his active life [7].

In 1927 the question of multi-partyism did not appear in the platform of the United Opposition. In 1935, however, having measured the consequences, Trotsky made a principle of it in The Revolution Betrayed and explained the fundamental reasons for it: "In reality, classes are heterogeneous; they are torn by inner antagonisms, and arrive at the solution of common problems not otherwise than through an inner struggle of tendencies". He thus broke clearly with the illusion of the homogeneity of the people which had dogged the revolutionary movement since the French revolution. And he converged with the historic warning launched in 1918 by Rosa Luxembourg: "Without general elections, an unhindered press and freedom of assembly, the free struggle of opinion, life in any public institution dies off, vegetates and the bureaucracy remains the only active element".

However his formulations on the role of the party remain quite ambiguous: "The proletariat can take power only through its vanguard [...] The proletarian revolution and dictatorship are the work of the whole class, but only under the leadership of the vanguard. The soviets are only the organized form of the tie between the vanguard and the class. A revolutionary can be given to this form only by the party". It is one thing to say that we have not up to now seen a victorious revolution without the intervention of a revolutionary party (whatever its name: movement, front, etc.). It is another thing to say that the proletariat can only come to power through its vanguard, if that means that it will exercise power by delegating it to this vanguard. What is then involved is the substitution, under cover of organically adequate representation, of the party for the class.

The probability of such an interpretation is reinforced by the following sentence. If the Soviets "are only the organized form of the tie between the vanguard and the class", they are not the sovereign organ of a new power that is destined to wither away, but the simple mediation between a class that is a minor and the party which incarnates the fullness of its delegated consciousness. The exception imposed by the civil war then seriously risks becoming the rule, to the detriment of self-emancipation.

A Premature Revolution?

Trotsky also undertakes to refute criticisms on two fronts: the Menshevik (and reformist in general) thesis according to which the worm was in the fruit of a premature revolution which was trying to artificially force the course of history; and the anarchist thesis according to which the bureaucratic degeneration came from an original "statist socialism".

For the former, as for Kautsky, the conditions were not ripe for a socialist revolution in Russia. Similarly, for Francois Furet, impatience and "revolutionary passion" won out over historical reason. And bureaucratic totalitarianism was just the foreseeable punishment for this original sin. This rhetoric about the event which must come in its time, just in time, neither too soon nor too late, belongs to a determinist logic of the meaning of history, of the notion of progress and of linear time.

The Russian Revolution was thus condemned to monstrosity from the October insurrection onwards by a "premature" historical birth, whereas the "objective conditions" of going beyond capitalism did not yet exist: instead of having the wisdom to themselves limit their aims, the Bolshevik leaders were the evil geniuses of this fatal error. It is as if, between July and October 1917, as the war continued, what was involved was a rational choice about the right historical tempo, a reasoned choice between a civilised British-style parliamentarianism and the dictatorship of the proletariat, and not a desperate confrontation between revolution and counterrevolution.

Moshe Lewin reminds us, as did Trotsky in his *History of the Russian Revolution*, how the Cadets, the Mensheviks, and the whole democratic centre then collapsed under the weight of antagonisms that no one controlled. Every crisis offers a choice. In 1917, the bankruptcy of the Kerenskys, the Miliutovs, the Tseretellis, laid bare the confrontation between the Kornilov reaction and Bolshevik revolution. Those were then the terms of the alternative. From a revolutionary point of view, wrote the great Soviet historian Mikhail Guefter, himself a victim of Stalinist repression, "there was no choice": "Having thought a lot about this problem, I can allow myself a categorical answer.

What was accomplished was at that time the only solution opposed to a more bloody change and to a senseless debacle. The choice came afterwards, a choice involving not the social regime, not what historical road to follow, but a choice within this road.

There were neither different readings nor steps that had to be mounted in order to reach the summit, but a junction, a choice of roads" [8]. Blanqui would have said, a fork. And these choices of what road to take are visible. They are called the NEP, the end of the civil war, the German Revolution, forced collectivization, the struggle against Nazism, the Chinese Revolution, the Spanish Revolution...

The worst, in this way of reasoning about "history at a snail's pace" is that these advisers of the 25th hour draw on their own cowardice and their own passivity to accuse of excessive haste those who accepted the challenges that were imposed by the situation. In reality the Bolsheviks were faced with the alternative: either revolutionary audacity or being crushed by the White reaction. But they situated this audacity within a strategic horizon that was European and international, staking everything on a rapid extension of the revolution in Germany and in the West, without which, as Trotsky again stressed, "Bolshevism will be liquidated" and the Soviet regime "left to itself will fall or degenerate".

The social convulsions that followed the war in Austria, in Hungary, in Italy, in Germany, show that it wasn't a question of unreasonable speculations, but a serious strategic hypothesis. Only historians of the accomplished fact and fatalist politicians claim that only what actually happened could happen.

Amputating real life of its multiple possibilities, they deprive politics itself of any strategic dimension, reducing it at best to a pedagogical task and most often to a powerless administrative accompaniment of the "natural" course of events, as if history was a long tranquil river, flowing, with a just a few regrettable delays, in the direction of inevitable progress. It is this lullaby of the philosophies of history that Walter Benjamin denounced in his Theses on the Concept of History, rightly accusing it of having been partly responsible for the paralysis of the German proletariat in the face of the rise of Nazism.

The paradoxical thing, which was correctly noted by Trotsky, about this rhetoric of resignation, is that they attribute at the same time to the party the role of an all powerful demigod: passive and objectivist materialism on the one hand, subjectivism and idealism on the other.

Bolshevism thus becomes the black sheep, guilty of this whole historical tragedy. Trotsky underlines on the contrary that while considering the party as a very important factor in the struggle, indeed the decisive factor in a particular extreme conjuncture, a revolution remains the combination of many causes and factors. And "the conquest of power, important it may be in itself, by no means transforms the party into a sovereign ruler of the historical process".

Contrary to what is often claimed, theory is not a determinist or teleological philosophy of history. If it is applied in order to understand the logics that are at work and the conditions in which what is possible would be either a revolution or a theological miracle, it does not claim to foresee the course of history, as classical physicists foresee the mechanical consequences of an initial cause. Gramsci very wisely said that we can only foresee the struggle and not its outcome, which is by nature uncertain. All the more so as there is no revolution "just in time", which arrives punctually at the appointed hour.

As Engels had already understood in his analysis of the revolution and the counterrevolution of 1848 in Germany, it is a question of the temporal dialectic of "already no longer" and "not yet". While freely criticising certain aspects of the Russian revolution, including the dissolution of the Constituent Assembly, Rosa Luxembourg paid the Bolsheviks the vibrant compliment of having "dared", of having seized the right moment (the kairos of the Greeks) to make a historical choice. It is those who at the decisive moment didn't dare that we should be calling to account. It is fashionable today to make revolutions responsible for all the catastrophes of the 20th century and to count their victims.

But who can say what was the price of failed revolutions and betrayed revolutions and what was the responsibility of those who when it was time to take the risk, slipped away? Who can say how costly for Germany and for Europe were the consequences of the aborted revolution of 1918-23 [9]?

The Morals of History

To the moralists who deliver their lessons by denouncing "the 'immorality' of Bolshevism", Trotsky replied in his 1937 pamphlet that "the moral qualities of every party flow, in the last analysis, from the historical interests that it represents".

But who determines and guarantees these interests? This temptation to ethical relativism has often been interpreted as a sort of vulgar Machiavellianism (or utilitarianism), according to which the end justifies all means. A year later, stimulated by his meeting with John Dewey, Trotsky came back to the question in a pamphlet that is often quoted, but not often read and badly understood, entitled Their Morals and Ours.

On the dialectic of ends and means, Trotsky is at the antipodes of a teleological justification: "if the end could justify the means we would have to look elsewhere for criteria for action: in heaven if not on earth! The theory of eternal morals cannot do without God. Absolute moral sense is only a timid pseudonym for God. It was the Jesuits who argued that the means in itself is indifferent and that its justification is determined by the end pursued. In this they prove themselves superior to the hypocrisy of the Church.

But in becoming bureaucratized these warriors of the church became in their turn downright rascals". In another form, the utilitarianism of Stuart Mill morally justifies the means by the pursuit of the common good. In the same way, with our contemporary partisans of ethical or humanitarian wars, the purity of the intentions (the defence of the rights of man or humanitarian interference) justifies the most dubious means, the ethical ideal justifies the worst armed terror.

What justifies the end? asks Trotsky on the contrary. In reality, if morals do not come from heaven, if they are embedded in social relations, "the end also requires justification". The vice is inherent in the formal separation between ends and means. What Nietzsche called bourgeois "moraline" thus becomes trapped in a logical impasse. Unlike readers who are in a hurry, Dewey very well understood Trotsky's arguments on the interdependence of ends and means and he avoided accusing him of cynicism.

If the ultimate criterion of concrete morality was, as Trotsky affirmed, not even the interest of the proletariat, but the universal development of consciousness and of culture (of which the proletariat was only the particular mediation), in other words what frees a humanity that is really human from its religious and social alienation, then all means are not permitted, even to a revolutionary infidel.

But, objected Dewey, when Trotsky, believing that he was historicising moral judgement and eliminating any abstract transcendance, made the class struggle the deciding authority in questions of morality, wasn't he transforming it, against his own intention, from a means among others into a supreme end? This well conducted controversy was unfortunately interrupted by the force of circumstances before Trotsky was able, as he had expressed the intention of doing, to follow it up.

The question of morality, like that of the revolution, presupposes the question of the dialectic, because if "Stalinism obviously came from Bolshevism, it did not come from it by virtue of formal logic but dialectically, not as its revolutionary affirmation, but as its Thermidorian negation".

More generally, if revolutions are followed by counterrevolutions, it is not because these are genealogically engendered, but from irreconcilable antagonistic opposition. Ignorance of the dialectic or its significant transformation into a formal logic of state as Stalinist reaction carried the day, prevented analyzing together the event and its conditions, the revolutionary moment and the process of social and cultural transformation, historical necessity and political contingency, ends and means, history and memory, what is real and what is possible. That is why, as Lukacs had well understood, "really revolutionary thought is impossible without dialectics", which is the very condition of any strategic thought and of a conception of history that is not positivist but strategic.

What is striking on re-reading the pamphlet Stalinism and Bolshevism in a quite different context, is the continuity of the terms of the polemic. To the crucial question that Mikhail Guefter asked again half a century later, whether there had been "a continuous march between October and the Gulag or if on the contrary was a question of two distinct political and moral worlds", the study of the

Stalinist counterrevolution gives a clear answer. Before the turning point of the 1930s, we can still speak of mistakes that could be corrected, of alternative orientations situated within the same perspective.

After that it is a question of antagonistic forces and projects which are totally opposed to each other. It is no longer a family quarrel which makes it possible to recover, a posteriori, yesterday's victims as disappeared witnesses of a "communist plurality" or to reunite under the same banner the zeks and their executioners. As Guefter again wrote, a rigorous periodisation makes it possible for historical consciousness to "penetrate the field of politics".

NOTES

[1] This can be found in Writings of Leon Trotsky, 1936-37, Pathfinder Press, New York, 1970 and online at the Marxist Internet Archive.

[2] Originally published in French by a collective of anti-communist intellectuals, the Black Book of Communism was published in an English translation in 1999 by Harvard University Press.

[3] Trotsky had just written a long article entitled "On the threshold of a New World War" (Trotsky, op. cit).

[4] As David King has demonstrated in a number of books of photographs. See in particular The Commissar Vanishes, Canongate, Edinburgh, 1997.

[5] Rene de Chateaubriand, Memoires d'outre-tombe, Paris, Flammarion, tome 3, p.647.

[6] Which was very well grasped by Hal Draper, Karl Marx's Theory of Revolution, vol. 4, Critique of other socialisms (Monthly Review Press).

[7] See the diary of Lenin's secretaries and also Moshe Lewin, *Lenin's Last Struggle*.

[8] Mikhail Guefter, "Staline est mort hier", L'homme et la societe. No. 2-3, 1988.

[9] See Pierre Broué , *La Revolution allemande*, published in English as *The German Revolution* (1998), first published by Porcupine Press, re-published by Historical Materialism books.

Notebooks for Study and Research

No.1 The Place of Marxism in History, Ernest Mandel (40 pp. € 5.00)

No.2 The Chinese revolution - I: The Second Chinese revolution and the Shaping of the Maoist Outlook, Pierre Rousset(32 pp. € 5.00)

No.3 The Chinese revolution - II: The Maoist Project Tested in the Struggle for Power, Pierre Rousset (48 pp. € 5.00)

No.4 Revolutionary Strategy Today, Daniel Bensaïd (36 pp. € 5.00)

No.5 Class Struggle and Technological Innovation in Japan since 1945, Muto Ichiyo (48 pp. € 5.00)

No.6 Populism in Latin America, Adolfo Gilly, Helena Hirata, Carlos M. Vilas, and the PRT (Argentina) introduced by Michael Löwy (40 pp. € 5.00)

No.7/8 Market, Plan and Democracy: The Experience of the So-Called Socialist Countries, Catherine Samary (64pp. € 5.00)

No.9 The Formative Years of the Fourth International (1933-1938), Daniel Bensaïd (48 pp. € 5.00)

No.10 Marxism and Liberation Theology, Michael Löwy (40pp € 5.00) [Out of print]

No.11/12 The Bourgeois Revolutions, Robert Lochhead (72pp. € 5.00)

No.13 The Spanish Civil War in Euzkadi and Catalonia 1936-39, Miguel Romero (48pp. € 5.00)

No.14 The Gulf War and the New World Order, André Gunder Frank and Salah Jaber (72pp. € 5.00)

No.15 From the PCI to the PDS, Livio Maitan (48pp. € 5.00)

No.16 Do the Workers have a Country?, José Iriarte "Bikila" (48pp. € 5.00)

No.17/18 October 1917: Coup d'état or Social Revolution, Ernest Mandel (64pp. € 5.00)

No.19/20 The Fragmentation of Yugoslavia: An Overview, Catherine Samary (60pp. € 5.00)

No.21 Factory Committees and Workers' Control in Petrograd in 1917, David Mandel (48pp. € 5.00)

No.22 Women's Lives in the New Global Economy, Penny Duggan & Heather Dashner (editors) (68 pp. € 5.00)

No.23 Lean Production: A Capitalist Utopia?, Tony Smith (68 pp. € 5.00)

No.24/25 World Bank/IMF/WTO: The Free-Market Fiasco, Susan George, Michel Chossudovsky et al. [Out of print]

No.26 The Trade-Union Left and the Birth of a New South Africa, Claude Jacquin (92 pp., € 5.00)

No.27/28 Fatherland or Mother Earth? Essays on the National Question , Michael Löwy (108 pp., €16, £10.99, $16)

No.29/30 Understanding the Nazi Genocide: Marxism after Auschwitz, Enzo Traverso (154 pp., €19.20, £12.99, $19.20)

No.31/32 Globalization: Neoliberal Challenge, Radical Responses, Robert Went (170 pp., €21.00, £13.99, $21.00)

No.33/34 The Clash of Barbarisms: September 11 and the Making of the New World Disorder, Gilbert Achcar (128 pp., €15.00, £10.00, $15.99)

No.35/36 The Porto Alegre Alternative: Direct Democracy in Action, Iain Bruce ed. (162 pp., €19.20, £12.99, $23.50)

No.37/38 Take the Power to Change the World, Phil Hearse ed. (144 pp., €9, £6, $12)

No.39/40 Socialists and the Capitalist Recession with 'Basic Theories of Karl Marx', Raphie De Santos ed. (216 pp., €9, £6, $12)

No.41 Living internationalism: A history of the IIRE, Murray Smith & Bertil Videt eds. (108 pp. €5, £4, $8)

No.42/43 Strategies of Resistance & 'Who are the Trotskyists?' Daniel Bensaïd (180 pp. €9, £6, $12)

No.44/45 (Forthcoming in 2010) The conflict in Palestine, Cinzia Nachira ed.

To order, email iire@iire.org or write to International Institute for Research and Education, Lombokstraat 40, NL-1094 AL Amsterdam.

Lightning Source UK Ltd.
Milton Keynes UK
04 February 2010

149538UK00001B/12/P